SARAH OCKWELL-SMITH

BETWEEN

A guide for parents of
eight- to thirteen-year-olds

PIATKUS

PIATKUS

First published in Great Britain in 2021 by Piatkus

1 3 5 7 9 10 8 6 4 2

A CIP catalogue record for this book
is available from the British Library.

ISBN 978-0-349-42777-5

Typeset in Stone Serif by M Rules
Illustrations by Rodney Paull
Printed and bound in Great Britain by Clays Ltd, Elcograf S.p.A

Papers used by Piatkus are from well-managed forests
and other responsible sources.

MIX
Paper from
responsible sources
FSC® C104740

Piatkus
An imprint of
Little, Brown Book Group
Carmelite House
50 Victoria Embankment
London EC4Y 0DZ

An Hachette UK Company
www.hachette.co.uk

www.littlebrown.co.uk

The information given in this book is not intended to replace
any advice given to you by your GP or other health professional.
If you have any concerns about your child's health, physical
or mental, contact the appropriate health professional. The
author and publisher disclaim any liability directly or indirectly
from the use of the material in this book by any person.

To my children, for teaching me how to be patient throughout the tween years. And to my parents, for putting up with 8- to 13-year-old me.

Contents

The Bridge Between Two Worlds

'We were still children, for all that we thought we weren't. We were in that in-between place, the twilight between childish things and grown-up things.'

Lost Boy: The True Story of Captain Hook,
CHRISTINA HENRY

Time passes in the blink of an eye. Surely it was only yesterday when that warm, mewling bundle was placed in your arms, eyes fixing on yours with all the intensity and knowing of an old soul who has lived many times before, yet in a tiny body, so fragile and new. Through sleepless nights and weary days, you came to know each other. Your world and your priorities shifted, and you slowly assumed a new identity that centred upon your child. A child who orbited you like a satellite, with you the safety of a home planet and the constant pull of gravity keeping you tied as one. Their dependence on you sometimes felt so very heavy, so all-consuming, and there were days (and many nights) when you reminisced and wished for your carefree past.

Oh, how appealing were thoughts of being able to sleep without little limbs starfishing next to yours, to visit the bathroom alone or eat in peace.

As weeks became months and months rolled into years, the sweet, busy, joyous and sometimes claustrophobia-inducing toddler years, in which a little sticky hand permanently reached for yours, gave way to the early school years. Full of glitter, junk modelling, phonics books and a plea for one more bedtime story. Then bam, before you can take a breath, you catch a glimpse of your child as the teenager they soon will be. A certain way they hold their jaw, peer through their impossibly long eyelashes or throw their head back as they laugh. And all at once, you realise that baby is no more. That child is fast becoming grown. Yet, they are not quite there.

Life is now a strange dichotomy of big parenting (my term for raising more mature, physically larger children with more complex problems and emotional needs) and little parenting (raising small children with physically exhausting, yet relatively simple needs). This is the world of the in-between. The bridge between two worlds. Not yet a teen, but not completely a child either. The between years are bittersweet: the loss of early childhood and yet the promise of such a bright and open future; mourning their baby days, while enjoying the thrill of looming independence. These times can be confusing, not only for your child but for you, too.

The in-between – or 'tween', as many refer to them – years of childhood are a unique period of development often overlooked. Advice abounds from multiple sources for the first five years of parenting, the beginning of childhood, you may say, yet it starts to tail off when children start school. It is true that once they are well settled at school, you often have a smooth ride parenting-wise for a couple of years, with the challenges of toddlerhood well behind you and those of the teen years far in the future. While ages five to seven may lull you into a false sense of security, it soon becomes apparent that around the age of eight, new challenges start to appear, as the outside world increasingly influences children, their behaviour and their relationships with others and themselves. It is often at this point that parents reach out for help and advice as they struggle to understand their children. A year or two later, as your child's age reaches double digits, things change again as puberty really starts to kick in, with all the emotional and physical issues that accompany it. And once puberty is well established and the teen years are imminent, the challenges of parenthood change yet again, with a new quest for independence, changing schooling, friendships and peer interactions bringing fresh concerns.

The tween years finish at age thirteen, when your child is officially a teenager, and help and advice for parents picks up once again. Despite the age demographic label changing on your child's thirteenth birthday, however, not much changes emotionally or physically for at least the first couple of teenage years (something we will look at in more detail in Chapter 1). You could argue that there is little difference between an older tween and a teen, aside from the label.

The middle years of childhood tend to be overlooked entirely, with a black hole of information until the teenage years – thirteen plus, the last years of childhood. When I was a parent for the first time, I often wondered if people thought that these in-between years – those between eight and thirteen – were inconsequential and uneventful. Did the lack of age-specific advice mean that nothing much happened in these years?

On the contrary – the tween years are some of the busiest developmentally and often the most challenging for many parents. Raising a tween can often leave you feeling like a parenting beginner all over again. The child you knew so well seems to change so rapidly, fluctuating almost daily. This middle period of childhood can be difficult for both parent and child. New behaviours surface, giving you the same worry and confusion you felt as a new parent all over again, only without the support that you had during the baby and toddler years. Even though we all went through this transition ourselves, it can be hard to access our memories and even trickier to recall information we may have learned in school biology lessons many years ago.

Despite these new challenges and changes, there is so little information available to help you on this journey. This book is aimed specifically at filling this gap – your handbook as you cross the bridge from childhood into adolescence, together with your child. It is the book I wish I had read when I was in your position.

Of course, the tween years span a relatively large time frame – five years, to be precise. While some of the information contained here is specific to a certain age bracket (about puberty, for instance) most is applicable to all ages within the tween years. In fact, a lot of the information will see you well into the teen years, too. If you do come across something that is a little more advanced than where you are with your child right now, you may choose to revisit that section in the coming years. Similarly, if your child is at the older end of the tween age scale, you may want to skip over a few sections that are aimed at slightly younger children.

The problem with 'the youth of today'

Have you ever noticed how our society is mostly kind and accepting towards younger children? So long as the child is small and cute, that is. When children approach adolescence (a term technically used to describe the period from the onset of puberty through to adulthood), acceptance and tolerance wane hugely. It is much harder to find a child cute if they are taller than you, I guess. And I think in many people's minds, size correlates with cognitive ability and emotional development – the presumption being that if a child is beginning to resemble an adult physically, they should behave like one, too. Unfortunately, this is not the case (something we will explore at length in Chapter 1), and this common misconception can lead adults, particularly those from older generations, to frequently admonish 'the youth of today'.

Tweens and teens are often labelled as lacking respect, particularly for their elders, and as being unruly in their behaviour. But these views usually tell us more about the person holding them than they do about our children. Clearly, they represent some form of memory bias, with adults remembering their own qualities at that age with a more positive slant; and they may also tell us a lot about how these people were themselves parented. Research has shown that adults who had a strict authoritarian upbringing are far more likely to find fault with today's tweens and teens.[1] But the youth-of-today phenomenon is not new. Adults have been complaining about tweens and teens for centuries, and likely will do for many more to come.

As it happens, the youth of today are no worse than their predecessors. In fact, there is evidence to show that adolescents today are considerably better in many ways than those from previous generations: rates of smoking, underage drinking, drug use,[2] antisocial behaviour and teen pregnancies[3] have fallen, while academic achievement, concern for the environment and acceptance of diversity have risen. Today's youth are, in fact, something to celebrate, rather than lament. How exciting that we are the generation raising them!

Building a strong, secure and open bridge

My aim in writing this book is to provide you with the information you need to help your child traverse the bridge from childhood to adulthood, while being mindful of your own needs, too. Your child still needs you to help them to feel secure and to steer them on their journey. Your input will help to reinforce this bridge and to grow the independence and confidence they require for the future. Importantly, your relationship during this period will help to keep both the entrance and exit of this bridge open, allowing your child to cross back over to you when they most need you. All the backwards and forwards, toing and froing are characteristic of this stage: little parenting, blending with big parenting, dependence meeting independence, holding on and letting go. Your openness and support during these years are key to building the relationship that you will have with your child in the future.

Throughout this book, we will constantly examine your relationship with your child and why it matters so very much, especially in Chapters 2 and 3, where we will discuss common problematic tween behaviours and what tweens really want (and need) to grow into happy and secure teens and adults. The relationship you have with your tween also provides the foundation for their future relationships with others. However, as they grow, they will often encounter difficulties in these new relationships – Chapter 4 looks at friendships in the tween years and what you can do as a parent when they don't run smoothly. Chapter 5 delves into your tween's relationship with themselves and how to encourage good mental health, now and in years to come. Finally, on the relationship front, Chapter 6 looks at romantic associations, consent and diversity in sexuality – subjects it's never too early to discuss with your tween, yet which are often delayed and avoided by so many.

Later in the book, we will move on to hot topics surrounding the tween years and issues commonly raised by parents. Chapter 7 delves into body image and why the tween years are key to helping your child grow into an adult with good body acceptance – one who is more likely to escape the seemingly ever-growing pressures of the diet and cosmetics industries. Chapter

8 considers personal hygiene and how to encourage tweens to understand and take care of their own bodies (including preparing for menarche – more commonly known as the onset of periods).

In Chapter 9, we focus on raising tweens who will advocate for others, and how to cultivate in them an empathy for the world around them and a willingness to change the world that they live in for the better (rather than changing them to fit into our current world). Our tweens are our future, so we should raise them to know that they matter, and that they can make a difference to whatever cause they choose to devote themselves to.

No book about tweens would be complete without a chapter on screen time, or 'how to get your child off their games console' and Chapter 10 is just that. This generation is growing up online more than any before. We can't escape the lure of screens and their influence over almost every element of our lives. Raising tweens to be screen savvy – to utilise the amazing possibilities that they present, while avoiding common pitfalls – is so important.

Chapter 11 looks at schools – at motivation, homework and academic and other achievements. The transition to secondary (or high) school is a huge milestone in the life of a tween and one worthy of some discussion. Chapter 12 is all about financial literacy, which I believe is vitally important; yet it's something that is just not discussed with tweens in our society. Classes about how money and debt work are completely absent from the school curriculum, but may be one of the most valuable life lessons you can give them.

Chapter 13 is the final chapter, which is no coincidence. It feels right to leave you at the age when your child becomes a true teenager – the official end of the tween years. Parting is the theme of this chapter: how to let go and give your child wings to fly (especially when you feel like holding on tight) is something many struggle with. How much independence is too much, or too little? And how do you cope with your own feelings as your child reaches towards looming adulthood. Although this book is about your tween, it is also about you as a parent, and it feels fitting to end with a chapter that concerns you as much as your child. After all, you will always be standing at one end of that bridge, watching with pride as your child continues their journey through the in-between, but ready and waiting with open arms should they need to return to you again.

Chapter 1

Tween Biology – Changing Brains and Bodies

'Many cognitive psychologists see the brain as a computer. But every single brain is absolutely individual, both in its development and in the way it encounters the world.'

GERALD EDELMAN,
American biologist and Nobel Prize winner

When I had my first baby – a boy, in 2002 – almost all tricky behaviour that occurred after toddlerhood was blamed on hormones. When he was four years old, I was told his boisterous and sometimes difficult behaviour was caused by a 'testosterone surge', yet there is no evidence to support the existence of such a thing. When he turned eight years old, again I was told that his change in behaviour was due to 'a rush of hormones'. I frequently see and hear comments like these in parenting discussion groups and forums. The general consensus seems to be that boys are swimming in a sea of testosterone as soon as they are out of nappies, which makes them behave erratically, rudely and aggressively, while girls receive an avalanche of oestrogen somewhere around their seventh birthdays, which turns them into stroppy, sulky, stubborn creatures. Neither of these beliefs is correct.

Hormones can – and do – influence behaviour; however, the impact is insignificant compared to that of the developing brain. If we must look to something to blame for behaviour in the tween years (although this is not something I advocate), it should be the remodelling of their brains. For this reason, I have chosen to start this book with a quick tour of brain development in the tween years. The more I've learned about this, the more the penny has dropped: this was why my children acted in the way they did! It had nothing to do with my parenting and little to do with hormones – it was all about their amazing brains. Understanding some basic neuroscience is incredibly freeing when you are a parent to tweens, and I hope that after reading this chapter you will find the same peace that I did.

Of course, we can't dismiss those hormones entirely. Puberty is a huge event, and despite having gone through it themselves, I find most parents are lacking in knowledge – not great when you are expected to be the expert and help guide your tween through the process. This is why the second half of this chapter is devoted to understanding puberty: when it happens, what happens, what signs to look for and what to do if things don't seem to be following a standard pattern.

Brain development in the tween years

Your child's brain has undergone tremendous development since they were a newborn. The most rapid period of neurological development occurs during the baby and toddler years. At birth, a human brain is around a quarter of its fully grown adult size and reaches three-quarters of its final size by the third year of life (although despite the dramatic increase in size in the early years, the brain is by no means fully matured until well into the twenties). This section will look at the most important neurological changes that occur during the tween years and how they impact your tween's behaviour.

Synaptogenesis

In infancy, a child's brain goes through a rapid process of development known as exuberant synaptogenesis. Synaptogenesis describes the process where new synapses (connections) are formed between the brain's neurons (nerve cells). A child's brain contains its peak number of synaptic connections around their third year of life, with around 15,000 synapses for each neuron. This number drops by around half over the next five years. Then a second surge of synaptogenesis occurs during adolescence, specifically just before puberty,[1] although this time the changes are not as fast as they were during the first three years of life. The brain continues to 'wire up' far beyond the teenage years and into the mid- to late twenties, and while the brain doesn't change much in size from around the fifth year of life (when it is almost at its adult size), connectivity is greatly increased as the child grows. This change in brain connectivity has a direct impact on behaviour, specific to the areas of the brain that are changing – a concept discussed a little later in this chapter.

Myelination

Myelination is the process by which the wires (or, to give them their correct name, axons) in the nervous system are protected, a little like an electrical wire being covered with insulation material, except that the brain's protection comes in the form of a fatty sheath, called myelin. Myelination allows the brain's electrical impulses to speed up and become more efficient. But the big difference between electrical-wire insulation and myelination is that an electrical wire is covered by one long insulation sleeve, whereas axons are covered by many individual sheaths of myelin, with tiny uninsulated gaps in between, known as nodes of Ranvier, which help to conduct nerve impulses quickly. Myelin is not only important for brain conductivity but also for physical movement and motor and sensory function. Myelination starts during the last few months of pregnancy and continues after the birth, peaking during infancy. The acquisition of new skills, such as learning to walk and talk, coincides with the number of axons being covered by myelin sheaths. Research has shown that myelination occurs last (not until the late teen years or even early twenties) in the frontal lobe – the part of the brain responsible for complex, logical and rational thought processes and behaviour[2] – which means tweens have uninsulated, or slower, connections in that area.

Plasticity and synaptic pruning

The term plasticity is used to describe the brain's ability to adapt to different environmental challenges and significant neuronal changes that occur as a result, giving way to new skills. This process enables tweens to adapt to, and learn from, their environments; however, if a tween encounters a new and potentially dangerous situation, their lack of brain development can inhibit them from acting in a logical and rational way. The process of plasticity that essentially aids the growth of independence in childhood, also inhibits it while under development and can often lead tweens to make incorrect and risky choices.

Synaptic (or neural, as it is sometimes called) pruning describes the process by which synaptic connections and extra neurons that are infrequently used are removed (pruned) in order to create a more efficient brain, leaving only connections that are used a lot. Often, synaptic pruning is referred to as working on a 'use-it-or-lose-it' principle. Pruning begins at the back of the brain, with the frontal part (the prefrontal cortex) the last to be pruned. While the earlier stages of synaptic pruning are directed by genetics, in later years they are controlled by the child's experience of the world around them and the stimulation that their brain receives as a result. Synaptic pruning, or rather the lack of it during the early tween years, has the effect of some-times slowing down your tween's logical thinking and rational actions; it is not until they are a good few years older that their brain's wiring will be stripped down to the most streamlined and most efficient version. The diagram below indicates a typical process of neural pruning during childhood and adolescence.

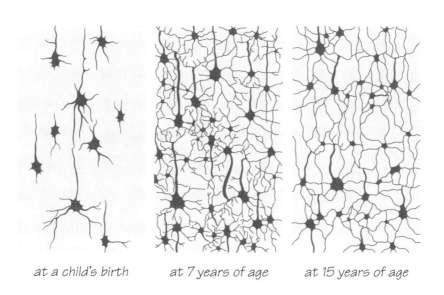

at a child's birth   *at 7 years of age*   *at 15 years of age*

Neurotransmitters

The tween brain is aided in maturation by three specific neuro-transmitters (chemicals which tell the cells in the brain what to do). These are: dopamine, serotonin and melatonin. The table below explains their main functions.

Dopamine[3]	Serotonin[4]	Melatonin[5]
Influences the experience of pleasure and pain.	Acts as a natural mood stabiliser.	Regulates the body's circadian rhythm (body clock) and encourages sleep.
Often known as a 'happy hormone', higher levels are related to increased feelings of happiness.	Involved in regulation of the sleep/wake cycle and appetite.	Levels increase during darkness (night) and decrease with light (day).
Levels believed to decrease during adolescence, often resulting in mood swings and difficulty with regulating emotions.	Fluctuations in levels during puberty can lead to mood disturbances and poor decision making.	Levels decrease as puberty progresses.
Can cause thrill- and novelty-seeking behaviour in adolescence, due to the reward of dopamine release.	Involved in behaviours and actions during emergency situations, as part of the fight-or-flight response (see page 118).	Also involved in the regulation of cortisol (stress hormone) levels and sexual functions.

A lot of tricky tween behaviour can be attributed to the changing levels of these chemicals in the brain, and the conscious (or usually unconscious) seeking of experiences that increase levels of them – for instance, the thrill of dopamine release that happens as a result of risky behaviour.

The Triune Brain model

The Triune Brain model, developed by American neuroscientist Paul D. MacLean,[6] is a simplified way to understand brain function and development. The word triune means 'three in one' and, accordingly, this model describes the brain as being composed of three main regions, as illustrated below: the reptilian brain (or the reptilian cortex), the mammalian brain (the limbic system) and the thinking brain (the neocortex).

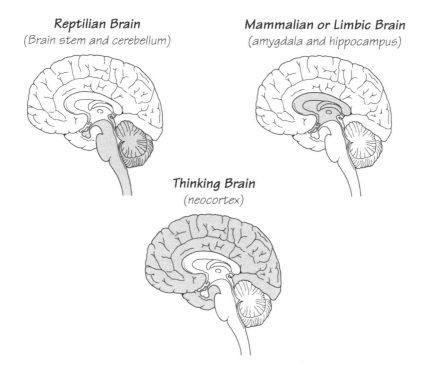

Reptilian Brain
(Brain stem and cerebellum)

Mammalian or Limbic Brain
(amygdala and hippocampus)

Thinking Brain
(neocortex)

The **reptilian brain**, consisting of our brain stem and cerebellum, is the part needed for our basic survival; it controls our essential bodily functions such as breathing, digestion, temperature regulation, circulation, hunger and thirst. The functions of the reptilian brain are automatic and this area is well developed and active from birth.

The **mammalian or limbic brain**, containing the amygdala and hippocampus, is the seat of emotions, giving us the capacity to feel and give love. The mammalian brain is also well developed at birth and in the early years of life.

The **thinking brain** consists of the prefrontal cortex, which makes up approximately five-sixths of the human adult brain. The prefrontal cortex is the home of so-called 'executive functions', such as critical and rational thought, planning and hypothetical thinking, working memory and impulse control. As we've seen, it is the final part of the brain to develop, in terms of neural pruning and connectivity. With complete development only occurring in the mid- to late twenties,[7] it is futile to think children will always think and act with logic and reasoning. And even when these attributes do begin to develop, it doesn't mean we should expect our tweens and teens to be able to access them. It is common for tweens to struggle with something 'in the moment', even though they would make a rational choice during discussion. For instance, if asked about retrieving a ball that has escaped into the road, most tweens would agree that it is silly and dangerous to this without first checking for cars. Yet, in the moment, when they find it hard to engage their thinking brain, they may well run straight into the road without looking.

Due to their underdeveloped prefrontal cortex, tweens (and teens) tend to use their mammalian or emotional brains (specifically the amygdala) for problem solving. In other words, our tweens are ruled by raw emotions, compared to the executive functions (particularly logic) that steer us as adults. A good example of this is to imagine a scene where your child has misplaced their school shoes: it's 8 a.m. on a school day, they are running late for the bus and their frantic search for their missing shoes quickly turns into an emotional meltdown, with sobbing and screaming. They get so caught up in their emotions that they cannot think rationally. They need you, as the adult, to step in with logic and calm, asking them to remember what they did with them when they came home from school the day before. This is the difference between them engaging the mammalian brain and you engaging the thinking brain. There is no point in chastising them for this emotional outburst – they can't change their brain or the processes by which their thoughts and actions are controlled.

As the frontal-lobe connections increase and grow in efficiency, children (and by 'children' here I really mean teenagers, not tweens) gradually move away from the raw emotional reactions of the mammalian brain and increasingly use the more sophisticated thinking brain. While you may think that this sounds preferable to the highly emotive behaviour you commonly see from your tween, it comes at a cost. The shift to the thinking brain means a move away from the mammalian brain and the emotional literacy it helps to provide. As a result, it becomes common for older tweens and teens to struggle with empathy and recognising feelings in others; they also tend to have less of a handle on their own emotions. A drop in empathy is important in the tween and teen years, as it enables our children to look inwardly – to work out who they are and who they want to become – without the pressures of others' thoughts and feelings influencing their self-discovery. In terms of recognising emotions in others, obviously this also requires a degree of empathy that our tweens just don't have. Therefore, it is common for them to misunderstand our intentions in our interactions with them. In the tween years, my own children would often say, 'Stop shouting at me!' when I hadn't ever raised my voice. What they perceived as anger on my behalf, was simply me trying to use logic to explain to them why something was inappropriate. This misinterpretation of the emotions of others is a common adjunct to the tween years.

Parents will often complain that their tweens are 'so self-centred' or that they 'seem blind to how others feel', and they frequently comment that 'their emotions seem so out of control'. These are all fair descriptions of the tween brain. But it absolutely does not mean that your child will remain so emotionally repressed for ever – it just means you have a normal tween, with a normal tween brain!

What does all this mean in reality?

In short, we shouldn't expect our tweens to be able to think, or act, like us, and we certainly shouldn't punish them for their incomplete brain development. As parents, we need to accept that we can't hurry these connections. But we can reset our expectations of our children.

So what should we expect? More thrill-seeking behaviour, more risk taking, looking to peers more often than their family for this buzz, lowered levels of rational and logical thinking, less impulse control, more mood swings, poor emotion regulation, misinterpreting the intentions of others and lowered levels of empathy. All things that are commonly blamed on the hormones released during puberty, when the changing tween brain is the real cause.

As we've seen, the tween brain is being continuously remodelled for at least the next ten years. New connections are being formed through synaptogenesis, the speed of the signals they emit are being honed through myelination and the processes of plasticity and pruning allow for these connections and signals to be as efficient as possible. In a sense, it's a little like planning a smart-house building project. The groundwork is there, as is the basic structure. The walls and roof are in place, the windows and doors are in, as are the solar panels to produce energy. The heating and lighting smart controls are mounted on the walls. Structurally, everything looks complete. Yet, what this project is missing is the high-speed fibre wiring and electrical insulation – the key ingredients that connect everything up, ensure the speed is optimal and tell it all what to do and how to act. You wouldn't expect all the smart-home features to work on day one, and we shouldn't expect our tweens to act as adults with adult wiring and neurological capabilities. They have a lot of work to go through before completion.

Chronotype shift – AKA 'goodbye early mornings, hello sleeping until lunchtime'

Do you remember the toddler years, when your child would be awake at the crack of dawn, raring to go at 5 a.m. every day, no matter what time they went to bed? Do you remember how you frantically researched ways to get them to stay asleep just a little longer? You probably invested in some heavy-duty blackout blinds and maybe a sleep-training clock. Remember the days when you wished that they would wake after you, so that you could get a little more desperately needed time in bed? Go back to that place now and hold those feelings with you – because the best way to get through what's going to happen to your child in the coming years is to keep reminding yourself of your longing for those early mornings to end. Gratitude is key to surviving the tween years sleep-wise – because soon your child will be almost impossible to rouse before lunchtime!

When I run toddler-sleep workshops and parents ask me how

to stop the early-morning waking, a little voice inside my head always chimes up: be careful what you wish for. Soon, your wish will come true – and then some.

Tweens and teens are commonly referred to as lazy. I don't just mean their reluctance to tidy up after themselves, but the fact that they want to spend half the day in bed. They also want to stay up later and later at night. As impossible as getting them up early in the morning is, getting them to bed at night is even harder. But this isn't due to laziness or stubbornness. It's the result of biology.

Puberty brings huge changes to sleep, not just because of behavioural changes and habits (more on this in Chapter 10, which is all about screen time), but because of shifts in a tween's circadian rhythm (commonly referred to as a body clock): they get tired later in the evening, hence the later bedtimes, and don't tend to wake until later in the morning (regardless of how much sleep they've had). This circadian shift, which corresponds to the onset of puberty and peaks in the late teens, results in a delay of sleep timings (both onset and waking) of anywhere between one and three hours.

The adolescent circadian shift is believed to be caused by a change in sleep homeostasis – i.e. the ability to stay awake for longer without feeling sleepy[8] – combined with a change in light perception at puberty, which influences the secretion of the sleep hormone, melatonin. This means that if your child naturally goes to bed at 7 p.m. and wakes at 6 a.m. before puberty, it's quite feasible that they won't want to go to bed until 10 p.m. or get up before 10 a.m. once puberty hits. Girls show signs of this circadian shift roughly a year before boys, which corresponds with starting puberty earlier. However, the magnitude of the chronotype shift is greater in boys,[9] and it is scientifically more likely that they will be harder to get out of bed in the morning (or into bed at night) during the tween and teen years.

The trickiest thing about the chronotype shift in adolescence is that people are largely ignorant of it. And adolescents being called 'lazy' is the least of their problems – a far greater issue is the structure of the school day. Most schools, particularly secondary or high schools, start the day at around 8.30 a.m. This means that most tweens realistically need to be up around 7 a.m. to get ready, eat breakfast and get to school on time. The trouble with this is that our tweens need to wake up well before their body clocks are ready. Or, in other words, every school day they are being woken biologically too early. This naturally results in overtiredness, as they find it hard to go to sleep early at night because of their shifted circadian rhythms. Add grumpiness, a brain that doesn't use much logic, and the resulting stressed parents, into this mix and you have a perfect storm.

Sadly, it's impossible to change a tween's natural chronotype; but it is possible to change what we do as a society. In the last decade, more and more research has been conducted into circadian shifts in adolescence and school-day starting times. One study found that delaying the start by just forty-five minutes resulted in better behaviour at school,[10] while a review of several studies echoed this finding and showed that a later start also resulted in less sleepiness at school, better academic achievement and even a reduction in car accidents (when children were old enough to drive).[11] As a parent, knowing that this circadian shift exists is incredibly powerful. Just like knowing about tween brain development, it enables you to reset your expectations of your child and empathise with them when they're finding things tough. We'll look at tween sleep (and how to handle it) in more detail in Chapters 7 and 10.

I hope that this section has helped you to understand what is happening in your tween's brain and shed some light on the potential causes of some of their behaviour. I think society is too quick to blame tweens – and their parents – for behaviour that is entirely normal for this age range and almost certainly a result of tweens' underdeveloped brains. For parents and carers, some knowledge of tween neuroscience is indispensable in helping to navigate these years. It isn't just your tween's brain that goes through enormous changes during these pivotal years though; their bodies do, too – often long before any physical differences are noticeable. So let's look at some of the key changes that may already be occurring for your tween, or will be soon.

The physiology of puberty

Puberty describes a period of development in which children's bodies sexually mature and become capable of reproduction. It is considered normal for puberty to commence at any point from the age of eight through to fourteen years of age. Girls tend to start puberty around a year earlier than boys, on average at the age of eleven. This time period sees many changes, both physical and hormonal and we'll look at these in turn.

Hormone changes of puberty

Puberty is controlled by hormones that are part of the hypothalamic–pituitary–gonadal axis (HPG axis, for short), which describes the parts of the body responsible for secreting certain hormones – specifically, the hypothalamus and the pituitary gland, both situated at the base of the brain and the gonads (ovaries and testicles).

The hypothalamus secretes something known as gonadotropin-releasing hormone (or GnRH for short) in what is described as a 'pulsatile' manner (in a regular pattern), sending a message to the pituitary gland, which triggers the release of follicle-stimulating hormone (FSH) and luteinising hormone (LH). FSH and LH then cause the gonads to make and secrete oestrogen and progesterone (in girls) and testosterone (in boys). Once these hormones are released, they feed back to the hypothalamus to ensure that levels remain stable.

In early childhood, before puberty, levels of FSH and LH in the body are low, due to slow activity of the GnRH pulse generator in the hypothalamus, and they do not stimulate the production of oestrogen, progesterone and testosterone. About a year before the physical signs of puberty are observed, GnRH pulse generation increases, resulting in an increase of LH and FSH which, in turn, triggers the synthesis and release of oestrogen, progesterone and testosterone, with the first physical signs of puberty appearing shortly after.

Adrenarche

A couple of years before puberty, between the ages of six and eight on average,[12] the adrenal glands (which are situated on top of each kidney) start to secrete hormones known as androgen precursors (such as androstenedione and dehydroepiandrosterone, or DHEA). These can later be converted to androgens (such as testosterone) through a process known as aromatisation. This androgen-precursor secretion takes place independently of the secretion of FSH and LH that occurs as part of the HPG axis activity during puberty. Androgens are commonly referred to as 'male hormones', although they are secreted by both sexes. Adrenarche affects cells in the body that produce hair, sweat and body odour. It is therefore common during adrenarche to notice a growth and sometimes darkening of body hair, sweat, body odour and a specific type of acne (spots) known as microcomedonal acne (small bumps most commonly found on the forehead and chin). Many mistake adrenarche for puberty, but it usually occurs a couple of years earlier and does not cause any other physical changes related to puberty, such as breast growth.

HOW MUCH DO THE HORMONES OF
ADRENARCHE AND PUBERTY IMPACT BEHAVIOUR?

How many times have you heard somebody blame their tween's behaviour on their hormones? So often, when asked on the internet about behaviour changes in eight-, nine- or ten-year-old children, parents will reply saying: 'Their hormones go haywire at that age; that's why their behaviour is so difficult!' There is little scientific evidence to support this belief, though. Research conducted in the USA in 2018 concluded that difficult behaviour during adolescence is not caused by hormones, but is rather coincidental.[13]

Does this mean that hormones, especially during puberty, have no impact on behaviour? Not necessarily. It is likely they do, just not as much as most people believe. It does seem that increasing levels of hormones, particularly testosterone, during puberty are linked to risk-taking behaviour;[14] but risk taking and perception of risk are also altered during adolescence due to brain development. So, once again, it seems wrong to point to hormones as the underlying cause when it's likely that the brain is just as much to blame – if not more so.

Physical signs of puberty

The physical signs of puberty are marked by something known as Tanner Stages (named after Professor James M. Tanner, who developed the measurement in England between the 1940s and 1960s).[15] Tanner Stages describe the appearance of secondary sexual characteristics. The sexual characteristics necessary for reproduction and present at birth (such as a penis and scrotum or vagina and uterus) are termed primary sexual characteristics, whereas those that are not directly required for reproduction (such as body hair, breast development and changes in muscle and fat distribution) are known as secondary sexual characteristics[16] and appear during puberty. Tanner Stages are used to assess the development of puberty, independent of age, with the earliest levels of development graded as stage 1 and the most mature levels graded as stage 5.

In boys, Tanner Stages look specifically at the following:

Development of external genitalia (penis, scrotum and testes)	Development of pubic hair
Stage 1: testicular volume less than 4ml (or less than 2.5cm long)	Stage 1: no pubic hair visible
Stage 2: testicular volume between 4 and 8ml (or between 2.5 and 3.3cm long)	Stage 2: downy pubic hair visible
Stage 3: testicular volume between 9 and 12ml (or between 3.4 and 4cm long)	Stage 3: very small amount of pubic hair visible
Stage 4: testicular volume between 15 and 20ml (or 4.1–4.5cm long)	Stage 4: pubic hair covering an entire triangle over the pubic region
Stage 5: testicular volume greater than 20ml (or greater than 4.5cm long)	Stage 5: pubic hair that extends beyond the groin on to the top of the thigh

In girls, Tanner Stages look at the following:

Breast development	Development of pubic hair
Stage 1: no feelable breast tissue	Stage 1: no pubic hair visible

Stage 2: can feel a breast bud under the areola

Stage 2: downy pubic hair visible

Stage 3: can feel breast tissue outside the areola (but with no areolar development)

Stage 3: very small amount of pubic hair visible

Stage 4: areolar development observed above the contour of the breast

Stage 4: pubic hair covering an entire triangle over the pubic region

Stage 5: further areolar development, now receding back in line with the rest of the breast contour; colour pigmentation changes and nipple protrusion

Stage 5: pubic hair that extends beyond the groin on to the top of the thigh

I find it much easier to understand Tanner Stages with some simple illustrations.

Tanner Stages for boys

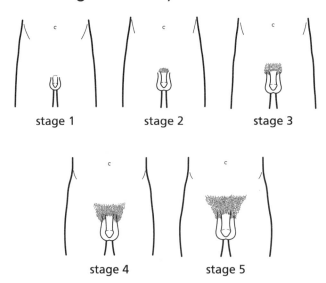

stage 1   stage 2   stage 3

stage 4   stage 5

Tanner Stages for girls

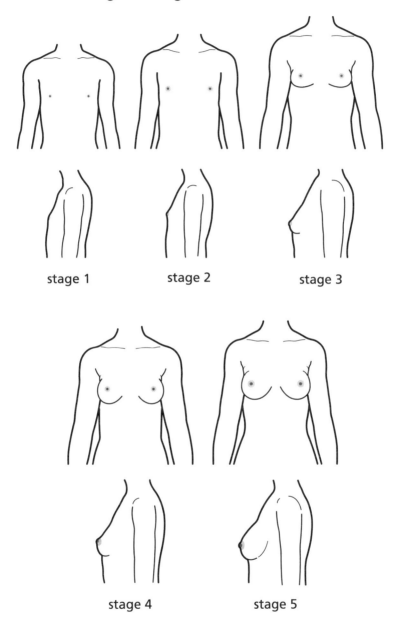

stage 1   stage 2   stage 3

stage 4   stage 5

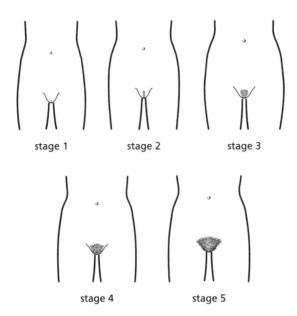

stage 1   stage 2   stage 3

stage 4   stage 5

Tanner Stages and average ages

There is a wide range when it comes to the timing of the different
Tanner Stages, as the table below shows:

Boys		**Girls**	
Tanner Stage	Age range	Tanner Stage	Age range
1	0–15 years*	1	0–15 years*
2	8–15 years	2	10–15 years
3	10–15 years	3	10.5–16 years
4	10–15 years	4	12–17 years
5	12.5–18 years	5	13–18 years

*Note: this stage runs from birth, as it is the pre-pubertal stage – the 0 isn't
a mistake!

*

Research has indicated that boys reach Tanner Stage 5 on average at fifteen years and six months, whereas girls reach the same stage on average at fifteen years and eight months.[17]

Menarche

Menarche, the medical term for a girl starting her periods, usually begins around two years after the first onset of puberty, when a girl enters the fourth Tanner Stage. Research has shown that the average age for menarche is somewhere between twelve and thirteen years of age, with the median age being twelve years and four months.[18] The menstrual cycle is often irregular during puberty, with bleeding lasting between two and seven days on average, and cycles lasting between twenty-one and forty-five days. Some cycles may be anovulatory (where no ovulation occurs). It can take up to three years for the menstrual cycle to establish into a mature pattern. We will look at preparing girls for starting their period in Chapter 8.

Voice breaking

As a boy grows, his larynx (or voice box) gets larger, while his vocal cords thicken and lengthen, making the voice sound deeper. Initially, while the body adjusts to these changes, boys can often have a squeaky or crackly voice – this is entirely normal and transient. The average age of voice breaking in boys is thirteen years and one month,[19] which is usually in Tanner Stage 3, before the development of full pubic hair.

Growth in height

Puberty is a time of rapid growth in children, with boys growing an average of 7.6cm per year. Girls tend to do most of their growing, height-wise, at the start of puberty and will only tend to grow 2.5–5cm per year after menarche. Boys, on the other hand, grow later in puberty, with peak growth happening usually between thirteen and fifteen years. Most girls are close to their adult height by the age of fourteen, whereas boys continue to grow for another couple of years, reaching close to their adult height at around the age of sixteen.

HOW TALL WILL YOUR CHILD BE?

A method commonly used to predict height in children after they have gone through puberty is known as the mid-parental height calculation. It considers the height of both parents and is thought to be accurate to within a range of almost 9cm. The calculations are a little different for girls and boys, as shown in the examples below.

For girls

Father's height minus 13cm. Add the remaining number to the mother's height and divide by two. As an example:

I am 155cm and my husband is 183cm.
So: 183cm – 13cm = 170cm
170cm + 155cm (my height) = 325cm
325cm ÷ 2 = 162.5cm

Therefore, my daughter's predicted adult height would be 162.5cm (5 foot 4 inches).

For boys

Father's height plus 13cm. Add the total to the mother's height and divide by two.

Using myself and my husband again:
183cm + 13cm = 196cm
196cm + 155cm (my height) = 351cm
351cm ÷ 2 = 175.5cm

Therefore, my son's predicted adult height would be 175.5cm (5 foot 9 inches).

Precocious or delayed puberty

Puberty that occurs significantly earlier or later than normal is medically termed precocious (for early) or delayed puberty.

Precocious refers to puberty that occurs before the age of eight for girls and nine for boys; delayed puberty is when it has not started before the age of thirteen for girls (in terms of breast development and if menarche has not begun by the age of fifteen), or by the age of fourteen for boys. We will focus on precocious puberty here, since this is more applicable to the ages covered in this book, and briefly touch on some causes of delayed puberty later in this chapter.

Precocious puberty – causes and incidence

Precocious puberty is further divided into two subtypes: central and peripheral. Central precocious puberty is the most common type and is diagnosed when puberty occurs physiologically normally (i.e. the HPG axis, pituitary gland and gonads secrete sex hormones), but too early. Often, the causes of central precocious puberty are unknown (in which case it is known as idiopathic central precocious puberty), although there is a genetic link, with puberty being more likely to start early if there is a family history on the father's side, indicating that a specific paternally inherited genetic mutation may be present. Obesity also increases the chances of precocious puberty. Some evidence has shown that the use of certain plastics (such as those containing bisphenol A and phthalates) heightens the risk of early puberty;[20] however, another review has disputed this finding. It is likely that exogenous (external) factors are involved somewhat, though. Central precocious puberty is estimated to affect between 1 in 5000 to 10,000 girls, with the condition being much less common in boys.[21] It is thought that of every ten children diagnosed with central precocious puberty, nine will be girls.

Peripheral precocious puberty is much rarer and occurs when the brain and pituitary gland are not involved in the start of puberty; instead, the cause is usually a localised abnormality involving the ovaries, testicles or adrenal glands, such as a tumour or cyst.

Diagnosis

If you suspect that your child may have precocious puberty, your first step should be to book an appointment with your family doctor. They should then refer you to a paediatric endocrinologist – somebody who specialises in hormones in childhood. They will conduct an examination of your child and order blood tests, particularly one to check the level of LH in your child's blood. They will also do something called a GnRH stimulation test, where an injection is given to stimulate the release of LH and FSH and blood is drawn at different times to measure gonadotropin levels. This test usually takes eighteen to twenty-four hours to complete. Alongside blood tests, it's likely that X-rays will be taken to assess growth (particularly of the hands) and further tests such as a pelvic ultrasound or head MRI (magnetic resonance imaging) may be needed to check for any possible underlying causes.

Treatment

Treatment for precocious puberty centres on addressing any underlying cause and giving medication – a GnRH analogue (which suppresses gonadotropin secretion) via an injection, nasal spray or implant to delay puberty until close to the time it usually begins. This helps the child to reach as close to their full adult height as possible and to avoid any emotional upsets that may accompany going through puberty at such a young age. Medication is more likely to be prescribed for those diagnosed at under seven years of age (whereas for children in whom puberty is just a year or so early, it may not be advised). When they reach the age of ten or eleven years, the medication will be stopped, and they will then enter full puberty as normal.

Long-term impact

Naturally, precocious puberty can worry parents, but its long-term effects (and those of treatment) are minimal. It can lead to a shorter adult stature and going through such a big transition at such a young age can cause emotional problems,[22] particularly in environments that are not set up to facilitate the transition to puberty (such as starting periods in infant- or early junior-school years). But no impact has been found on children's future fertility, from either the medication or the condition itself. There is some evidence that puberty-suppressant medication can cause issues with bone density and may make children more at risk of osteoporosis later in life, and there is still a lack of long-term safety data (from before the 1980s), but the medications given do appear to be largely safe.

Speaking on a purely personal level, I was diagnosed with idiopathic central precocious puberty when I was five years old. I was then very tall for my age, but not overweight, and my mother noticed unusual breast and pubic-hair growth. I was prescribed a GnRH analogue nasal spray until my tenth birthday, at which point I stopped the medication and my puberty started naturally shortly after, with menarche at age eleven. I honestly didn't find the experience emotionally distressing. In fact, I remember enjoying being the tallest in my school year until the start of secondary school (when I quickly became the shortest!). My only unpleasant memories are: first, having to stay in hospital once a year to have a GnRH stimulation test (at that time it was done with children as inpatients and only in one specialist hospital, in London, which meant an annual trip away from home); second, having an annual pelvic ultrasound and being made to drink lots of water and not go to the toilet all day (I wasn't good at that!), to ensure a full bladder for a clearer image; and third, the funny smell and taste of the GnRH analogue nasal spray I had to take every day (now injections and implants are more common). The only long-term effects have been my short stature and a potential bone-density issue. My height, using the mid-parental height calculation, should have been around 165cm; instead, I reached the lofty heights of 155cm.

Differences in sex development

For some children, puberty is different to the norm. Differences in sex development (or DSDs, for short) is a term used to describe a group of conditions in which a child's genetics, hormones or primary or secondary sex characteristics are atypical. DSDs shouldn't be confused with sexual orientation or gender identity.

Some DSDs are apparent from birth, with the appearance of what is known medically as ambiguous genitalia – those which do not appear to be either clearly male or female. One example of this is something known as congenital adrenal hyperplasia (CAH). In CAH, the adrenal glands that sit on top of the kidneys are unusually enlarged and there is a deficiency of an enzyme that stimulates them to make cortisol which, in turn, causes levels of androgens (male hormones) to be higher. At birth, babies with CAH can have mineral imbalances and baby girls can be born with male-looking genitalia. CAH can also affect children later in life, because of the increased androgen levels. Around puberty, girls can develop facial hair and experience voice breaking, earlier onset of puberty and an absence of periods. Boys may also go through an earlier puberty and have an enlarged penis and smaller testicles. Both boys and girls may initially seem tall for their age but end up shorter as adults because of their early puberty.

Other DSDs are not discovered until the child approaches puberty. Initially, the child may present with ordinary-looking genitals, but their sex development is different from the norm. Boys may be affected by something known as Klinefelter syndrome, where they are born with an extra X chromosome, resulting in the usual level of testosterone not being produced, so that secondary sex characteristics do not develop at puberty. Girls may be affected by Turner syndrome, where they are born with a missing X chromosome, which inhibits normal function of the ovaries and the development of secondary sex characteristics at puberty. Another DSD that may affect girls is Mayer-Rokitansky-Küster-Hauser syndrome, where girls are born with the usual external genitalia, but do not have a fully developed uterus, cervix (the opening to the uterus) or upper vagina (the inner muscular tube). As the ovaries are usually not affected, they will develop secondary sex characteristics at puberty, but no accompanying menarche; indeed, the lack of periods is often the first sign that a girl may have Rokitansky syndrome.

Not all delayed puberty is caused by a DSD, though. There may be other physical causes at play – for instance, side effects from medical treatment, such as chemotherapy.

As with precocious puberty, the best approach to handling DSDs with your tween is to be led by them. Give them autonomy and choice over any medical decisions that need to be made, including surgery, and be open and honest with them, avoiding hushed conversations about them with others. Respect, communication and openness really are key.

You can find resources for more information about DSDs, and support for tweens and families affected on page 243.

I hope this chapter has helped you understand a little more about the physiological changes involved in the tween years. It is certainly a time of huge growth and development, some of which we can see, and a lot that we can't. It is so important to remind ourselves that although we can observe that our children are slowly becoming more and more like adults physically, their brains are nothing like ours. We shouldn't expect adult-like behaviour from them, regardless of how grown-up they look. Blaming tween behaviour on hormones also does them a great disservice because the reality is that their brains are rapidly changing, and our misunderstanding of this development is what tends to cause most issues. This leads us nicely into Chapter 2, which is about our understanding of tweens and what they need (and want) from us.

Chapter 2

What Tweens Really Want (and What They Really Need)

'Above all, children need our unconditional love, whether they succeed or make mistakes; when life is easy and when life is tough.'

Barack Obama

When I announced I was writing this book on my social-media accounts, I was met by many comments from parents, exclaiming, 'Amazing', 'Can't wait', 'I would love to be able to understand my tween!' I hear this so often – parents complaining that they just don't understand their children; their needs and their wants as they get older. But it's a statement that always confuses me. You see, we've all been there. We've all been tweenagers. We all inherently know what it feels like. We know what we needed from our parents and caregivers at the time. We know what made us feel good and we know what made us feel bad. We each have such a rich internal parenting resource, and yet we so rarely use it. So while this chapter will explore common themes around what tweens really want and need, I genuinely believe that the best starting point for any parent is to reminisce and use those memories of their own past to empathise with their tween today.

Revisiting your own tween years

Close your eyes and let your memory drift for a moment. Can you remember a time from your own childhood, between the ages of eight and thirteen, when you felt particularly frustrated or let down by a parent or caregiver? (That caregiver could be a teacher, another relative or an adult who held a position of authority over you.) What led to those feelings? Was there one event – perhaps a conversation, something they said (however throwaway) – that made you feel hurt, angry or frustrated? Was it something they did – an action that caused such big feelings in you that it remains fresh today? Or perhaps it was something they *didn't* do? An inaction on their behalf at a time when you really needed them to do something. Can you imagine yourself inside your childhood body and think about what you needed from your parent or caregiver then? What did you need them to say, or do differently? Perhaps there wasn't one specific incident, but a series of small events – inconsequential alone, but impactful together – that shaped who you are today. What would you change about your parent or caregiver's response if you could turn back the clock?

When I work with parents on this exercise, I ask them to write down key words, or attributes they wish their parent or caregiver had had at the time and things they wish they had done. The following feature on almost every list:

- I wish they had really listened to me, rather than just speaking *at* me.

- I wish they had understood, and appreciated, my point of view more.
- I wish they'd appreciated my feelings, too.
- I wish they had made the time to be with me that I needed.
- I wish they had known what was really going on for me.
- I wish they had respected me more.
- I wish they could have put their own problems to one side sometimes, so they could help me with mine.
- I wish they had known that making me feel worse didn't make me behave better.

Perhaps your own list looks similar?

This list is a good starting point for developing a road map to help us deal with our own tweens. The best way to respond to these wishes is in the ways we wish we had been responded to when we were the same age.

The thing is that so many of us weren't always treated with understanding, respect and dignity by adults in our own child-hoods. And it can be so easy to subconsciously continue the same treatment and methods that we ourselves were raised with (and, in turn, those that our parents were raised with). Society constantly reinforces messages that children should be made to respect adults (usually through harsh, authoritarian methods) and that their voices are unimportant. If only we truly respected children, rather than simply demanding respect from them.

Very often, the behaviours and actions of our own children that trigger us so much are the same as those that we would have been punished, dismissed and chastised for as children. Although, deep inside, we all know what our tweens need – and know how we need to parent, based on our own childhood experiences – it can be so hard to break those conditioned responses. The good news, though, is that you've already jumped the first hurdle: realising they exist. So many adults exist in a state of cognitive dissonance when it comes to parenting: they don't consciously understand and accept (often because it is too difficult or painful to do so) that their own upbringings were sometimes less than optimal, and so they repeat the cycle, passing it from generation to generation. Awareness – or parenting consciously – is the first step to raising your children with the empathy and respect you wish you had been shown as a child.

When your tween's behaviour triggers you

Has your tween ever done or said something that has made you irrationally angry?

Children are commonly disciplined in ways to create compliance with adult wishes and commands. Simply, they are brought up to conform to adult expectations with little consideration of their own feelings. If you were raised to obey as a child (as many were), you may struggle with conflict with your children (and other adults), and the natural response to your tween questioning your authority, ignoring you or answering back is likely to be one of anger or frustration. But we must understand that our strong reactions to this are more to do with our own upbringings than our tweens' behaviour.

The next time your tween says or does something that makes you feel irrationally angry or frustrated, take a breath and ask yourself: 'Am I reacting consciously to my tween here, or are there are other factors influencing me?' Asking this question every time you feel triggered helps you to become more aware, separating your tween's behaviour from any conditioned responses you may hold in your psyche. The more you practise this, the better you will get at it. When you recognise that your reaction is because of your own trigger, and not necessarily something your child has said or done, you will be able to pause and act in a controlled and empathetic manner. In the next chapter, we will look specifically at ways to handle your feelings and emotions 'in the moment' when disciplining your tween. Additionally, if this section of the book throws up some big feelings for you, you may find it helpful to access some of the resources listed under 'Recovering from narcissistic parenting' on page 243.

Reliving the best parts of our childhoods

Just as we must consider the less-than-optimal features of our own childhoods, we should spend some time thinking about the best parts, too. Can you repeat the exercise on page 38, but this time close your eyes and think of a time when you felt really seen and respected by your parent or caregiver? What was it that they said, or did, that made you feel supported and understood? Once again, write down any key words or attributes that your parent or caregiver (again, this can also be a teacher, another family member or adult with authority) actually demonstrated. Unsurprisingly, this list usually looks remarkably similar to the list parents generate when I ask them how they wish their parent or caregiver had responded to them.

What do you hope to emulate from your own tween years with your children? Did you have a strong role model growing up? A parent who nurtured you and made you feel safe? An older sibling who encouraged you? A teacher who always took the time to check in with you and find out what you needed help with if you were ever stressed? Write a list of the positive traits, qualities and actions you would like to pass on to your tween (you can either use the space below or a notebook):

Parenting styles in the tween years: which is the most effective?

There is a mistaken belief that children need harsher parenting as they get older. I often read comments from those dismissing a respectful style of parenting saying, 'But the world is tough. You don't do children any favours by mollycoddling them. It's better to prepare them for the real world.' I think the assumption here is that when they are babies and toddlers it's OK to be kind to them, but as they get older, we should ready them for independence in the world by being less nurturing. This is such a ridiculous concept, yet it is a belief that seems to be widespread.

The role of parents is to provide a safe harbour for their children – a place where they can be themselves without fear of retribution, in order that they feel confident enough to withstand any negative treatment they may receive from the world when they are older. Chipping away at a child's confidence early on will only make them feel insecure and uncertain of their own voice. The best way to prepare children for the reality of the world is to give them the skills and resilience they need within the safety of their own homes, and this comes only when they are raised with empathy and respect. Providing a place where they can share all their emotions, without fear of ridicule or punishment, and where they will receive support for them, is the best way to prime children to go into the world with self-control and resilience. Perhaps also, we can hope to raise them to better the world for others, too.

Research into the impact of parenting styles has been popular since the 1960s, after the pioneering work of developmental psychologist Diana Baumrind and her Parenting Typology.[1] Baumrind described four distinct parenting styles. Let's look at each in turn.

Authoritarian/disciplinarian

Commonly described as 'Victorian' or 'Fear-of-God' parenting, this can best be summed up by the phrase 'Do as I say, not do as I do'. Children are expected to blindly follow the commands of adults, obeying whatever is asked of them. Respect for adults is demanded, yet it is rarely shown to children and certainly not earned by the adults in question.

The following are the key features of authoritarian parenting:

- It is highly demanding of children; parents expect of them behaviour that they are often incapable of developmentally.
- Boundaries are often overly strict and too many are imposed.
- Tricky behaviour is usually met with punishments of some sort, with little regard given to how age-appropriate these are.
- Empathy with children is often low and adults do not take time to uncover the big emotions underlying difficult behaviour.
- The approach is parent-centred: the adult knows best. Adults have little respect for children but demand a lot from them.
- Children are given little autonomy. The control is all 'owned' by the adults.
- Adults seek to change the behaviour of children but are rarely concerned with looking at their own.
- It tends to be less affectionate and less nurturing.

Permissive/indulgent

Permissive parents are often described as overindulging their children. They tend to be low on discipline with few rules and those they do have are often not reinforced. Permissive parents are seen as allowing their children to do whatever they want when they want, and are often described as being 'afraid to discipline, or as 'trying to be the child's friend, not their parent'.

The following are the key features of permissive parenting:

- Parents have low expectations of their child's behaviour, often dismissing difficult behaviour as 'just their age'.
- The child is often capable of better behaviour, but this is not encouraged through any form of teaching or discipline from the parents.
- Few or no boundaries or limits. Whatever rules the family do have are often not enforced when broken.
- Children can do whatever they like, whenever they like – they are given huge amounts of autonomy and control, even when it is inappropriate.
- Parents often grapple with their own emotions, and may not discipline for fear of upsetting their children as they can't cope with them when they are sad or angry.
- Parents are usually highly affectionate and very nurturing.
- Parents are highly responsive to their children's needs but can often misinterpret them or react in ways that are not beneficial in the long term (for instance, always 'giving in').

Uninvolved

Uninvolved parents are like permissive parents, only without the underlying affection, love and nurturing. Whereas a permissive parent will be slow to discipline because they don't want to upset their child, an uninvolved parent won't discipline because they can't be bothered to or have other things they would rather be doing.

These are the key features of uninvolved parenting:

- Children are given lots of autonomy; they can do what they want, while parents keep out of their way.
- Parents tend to show low levels of affection and nurturance towards children.
- Expectations of children and their behaviour are low and they are left to carry on doing whatever they want, regardless of how inappropriate their behaviour may be.
- Parents don't look for underlying causes of difficult behaviour and don't help children to solve problems.
- There are low levels of discipline – because parents don't really care what their children are doing – and few boundaries.
- Neglect.

Authoritative

Authoritative parents combine the best parts of authoritarian and permissive parenting, with none of the negatives. They are warm and nurturing, with realistic expectations of children and they discipline effectively, while remaining empathetic and understanding of them. This is a collaborative style of parenting whereby everybody's needs are respected.

These are the key features of authoritative parenting:

- Parents have age-appropriate expectations of their child's behaviour. They understand what they are capable of doing at each age and reset their expectations accordingly. Their parenting is informed and mindful.
- Parents set realistic boundaries and limits, with an awareness of the child's age and environment. They set just the right number of rules – not too many, but not too few.
- Rules and boundaries are always enforced, but respectfully and kindly.
- There is a good balance of control between parent and child: children are given the autonomy and freedom appropriate for their age and situation, and where needed the adult will step in and take control again.
- Discipline is always conscious (not just repeating what parents were raised with) and used in such a way that it teaches children how to behave better.
- Parents take time to understand the underpinning causes of difficult behaviour, and work with the child to resolve any problems.
- Parents understand that respect needs to be earned and they behave in a way that inspires it. The child is respected as well as the parent.
- Parents are mindful of the effects of their own emotions and understand that they need to be a good role model for their child. They seek to change their own behaviour as often as they do their child's.
- Parents show a high level of affection and nurturance and have a strong attachment with their child.
- Parents are highly responsive to the child's changing needs and seek to meet them wherever possible and appropriate.

- Parents are not afraid of upsetting their children when they reinforce boundaries and discipline; however, they always seek to help them with any difficult emotions that may follow.

By now, you have probably guessed that the authoritative style of parenting is considered the most effective and the least harmful, although I prefer to call it 'gentle parenting', as I find many parents confuse the term authoritative with authoritarian (plus, it's also a bit of a mouthful!).

In terms of the parenting style our tweens need most from us, authoritative is always the answer. Striving to be an authoritative, or gentle, parent can be hard though, especially for those who were raised in another style. If you were raised in an authoritarian house, it can be particularly hard to ignore behaviours that trigger you, because you yourself would have been harshly disciplined for them. Many parents who were raised this way can also slip into a more permissive style of parenting in a desperate attempt to avoid the same treatment they received as a child. This can often lead them to be scared to discipline or take control when it is necessary, for fear of fracturing their relationship with their child. There is no easy answer here; rather, it's a case of being aware of your natural tendencies and the reasoning behind them and consciously trying to change.

I also think it's important to hold up authoritative parenting as an ethos to aim for, rather than seeing it as a list of attributes and actions you must achieve every single day. Otherwise, you are doomed to fail. Even the best gentle parents will adopt another style occasionally, and that's OK, so long as you are aware and seek to change your actions in the future. What I'm really saying is that we are all a work in progress. No parent is perfect, and it is unrealistic to aim to be so. Be mindful of your predominant parenting style, but don't be too hard on yourself when you slip now and again. We're all human and, in many ways, it's good for your tween to see you mess up sometimes. The most important thing to do when you feel you are losing your way is, first, to apologise (it's OK to change your mind after you've said something to your tween, once you have had a chance to reflect) and, second, to learn from the experience. The journey your tween is on is as much your journey as theirs: you are learning together as you go.

Maslow's hierarchy of needs

Perhaps one of the most famous pieces of work looking at the physiological and psychological needs of humans of all ages is that of Abraham Maslow. His 'Theory of Human Motivation', published in 1943,[2] divided the needs of humans into five separate stages, each one building upon the other, with the most basic needs for survival coming first. The final stage, termed 'self-actualisation', was reached only if all the needs in the previous stages had been met. Self-actualisation was considered by Maslow to be the pinnacle of human development, achieved when a child felt safe, nurtured, accepted, supported and loved, with a sense of belonging, in addition to their more basic physical needs being met.

The illustration below shows the levels of Maslow's hierarchy as they would apply to tweens (although I have seen many memes shared on social media with another layer added to the very bottom, reading, simply: 'Wi-Fi'!)

If we consider Maslow's hierarchy from the point of view of an ideal parenting style, there is only one that fits well – that of the authoritative parent.

Containment

One aspect of parenting that authoritative parents are usually great at is supporting their tweens with big feelings and emotions, no matter how uncomfortable they may be for both. This support and sense of belonging and acceptance, regardless of how they feel or behave, is one of the steps to achieving self-actualisation in Maslow's work. The trouble is, when tweens are feeling big emotions and are acting out in particularly horrible and unlovable ways, it can be incredibly hard to be the adult and to provide this support when you are unconsciously triggered and predisposed to punish or shout and join them in their dysregulated feelings. Whatever the behaviour or underlying issue may be, however, your tween always needs the same from you: empathy and support. This means that you need to take a breath – physically and metaphorically – before responding as the adult in the situation. And that response needs to be such that you are calm enough and mature enough to take on board your child's big feelings and help to diffuse them, while 'holding space' to help them work out how to handle the problem.

This idea of holding space was described by the psychoanalyst Wilfred Bion in his theory of containment.[3] Bion described containment as a person's ability to take on board difficult emotions from another, transform them and then return them diffused. In terms of parents or carers and tweens, Bion would describe the parent or carer as the one doing the containing and conveying back a sense of calm and understanding, helping the tween to diffuse and manage their feelings and to find solutions; indeed, sometimes identifying the underlying problem, which may not be initially obvious to the tween.

When I run workshops with parents, I always use the analogy of storage containers to help explain Bion's work and how it relates to parenting. I describe buying a set of Tupperware containers to store my breakfast cereal in. I ask parents to imagine a big family-sized box of cornflakes and two Tupperware containers – one small (much too small to hold all the contents of the box) and the other large (with enough space for all the cereal). Then I ask them to imagine pouring all the cornflakes into the small container. If they kept pouring after the small container was full, cornflakes would spill out everywhere and make a huge mess. This, I explain, is a metaphor for their tween's brain. The small container represents their tween's level of brain development and ability to regulate emotions. The cornflakes are the everyday stresses and feelings they experience in the world. When the stressors outweigh a tween's brain's capacity to regulate, a big explosion occurs – not of cornflakes, but tantrums, tears, swearing, door slamming, backchat, sulking and hurtful words. Enter the large container – or the parent or carer. As adults, we have a much larger capacity for containment. Just as the large Tupperware container can hold the contents of a whole family-sized box of cornflakes, we have mature brains that can regulate our emotions and help us to regulate those of others, too. Simply put, when our tweens' containers are full, we have the space and the maturity to help them to carry the load and so lessen it a little.

Now, this would all work perfectly if we, as adults, were never at full capacity ourselves. But what happens if we were already full of our own cornflakes and we try to take on board our tweens' cornflakes, too. Here, I am referring to those things that make us feel 'full up', such as work stress, relationship and friendship worries, money problems, health troubles and all the demands of everyday adult life. When was the last time you said, 'I just can't take any more', 'I've had it up to the eyeballs', or 'I've had it up to here with . . . '? We commonly use words that describe ourselves as being full up. But if we are full up, we have no capacity to hold any of our child's emotions. Not only do we not help them when they are full, we can often make things worse, as we have our own explosions, too.

Understanding containment and the impact of allowing ourselves to get too full up, to the extent that we are incapable of containing our tweens' big feelings, is key in authoritative – or gentle – and effective parenting. As parents and carers, we must consciously seek to offload some of what fills up our containers and stop them from becoming too full, so that we can stay calm and be in a position to help our tweens with their troubles. If we don't do this, we will only make their behaviour worse by adding to it with our own poor emotion regulation. This is something we will look at more later in the book (see Chapter 13), with a focus on self-care for parents and carers of tweens to avoid this double explosion. For now, I will leave you with the picture of being mindful about not adding too many of your own cornflakes to your container, so you have space to contain those of your tween.

Be your tween's champion

Thinking back to Maslow's hierarchy and the different parenting styles, we know that in order to reach their full potential, our tweens need parents and carers who will help to lift them up and support them, especially when the rest of the world sometimes seems to be pushing them down.

Your tween needs you to be their champion. What do I mean by this? They need to know that you have their back and that even when it's hard for you, you will stand up for them, support them and ensure that they are treated with the compassion and respect that they deserve. Perhaps you will need to speak up for them in an education setting (see Chapters 5 and 11, where we discuss potential issues at school and difficulties with learning) or you may need to be your child's advocate with your own family or friends. Being prepared to stand up for and support your tween is key in letting them know that you will always be there for them. This, in turn, will make them far more likely to open up to you and ask for your help when they need it.

A QUICK GUIDE TO MEETING
A TWEEN'S EMOTIONAL NEEDS

If I am asked to summarise the best way to raise a tween, I will always ask parents to think about their own upbringings and tween years (as we did at the beginning of this chapter), because empathy always has to be the starting point – and what better way to empathise than imagining yourself in the same shoes. I will often explain authoritative parenting, too, and how tweens need good boundaries and discipline, but also a loving, compassionate parent or carer who is willing to contain their big feelings. If I were to summarise in just a few words though, I would pick only five. Together these words spell the word 'tween':

- **T**olerant
- **W**arm
- **E**mpathetic
- **E**mpowering
- **N**urturing

What do tweens need? They need tolerant caregivers who understand adolescent brain development, the physiology of puberty and age-appropriate behaviour. They need a warm relationship, focusing on attachment. They need buckets of empathy and containment, especially at times when they are acting in unlovable ways. They need us to empower them, by being their champions and giving them autonomy and freedom when appropriate. And finally, they need us to nurture them to full bloom, or as Maslow would say 'self-actualisation'.

What tweens wish their parents knew

When I started to research this book, I thought I had a fairly good idea about how tweens feel. After all, I was one once, and I also have four teenagers, so this stage of parenting is very fresh in my mind. Then I realised that I had made a huge mistake in assuming that I really knew how all tweens today feel. So I set out to speak to some of them, and I asked 100 tweens four specific questions:

1. What's one thing you wish your parents or carers understood, or said, more?

2. What's one thing you wish your parents or carers didn't do or say?
3. What do you think is the hardest thing about being your age?
4. What do you think is the best thing about being your age?

Their answers were insightful, and I would like to leave you with some of them to finish this chapter:

What's one thing you wish your parents or carers understood, or said, more?

- 'I wish they understood that sometimes something pops into my head and I just do it. I can't stop myself from doing it and I want my parents to understand that.'
- 'I wish they understood how important gaming is to me; it helps me relax.'
- 'I wish they told me that they're proud of me more.'
- 'I wish they understood that If I'm not happy, it doesn't mean it's their fault.'
- 'I wish they understood how I feel when I am nervous.'
- 'I wish they would say that I've done a good job more often when I do good things.'
- 'I wish they understood how annoying my sister can be sometimes.'
- 'I wish my dad would spend more time with me.'
- 'I wish they understood that when I get stressed, I don't like being asked questions.'
- 'I wish they'd ask "Are you OK?" or "How can I help more?"'
- 'I wish they understood that I don't like doing homework!'

What's one thing you wish your parents or carers didn't do or say?

- 'I wish they didn't get angry when I do things I don't mean to do.'
- 'I wish they wouldn't shout at me.'
- 'I wish that they didn't tell me "No" all the time.'
- 'I wish they wouldn't play on their phones so much.'
- 'I wish that my dad was nicer to me when I feel annoyed. He shouts at me and it makes me mad. Mum is kinder when I'm angry; she knows how I feel and makes me feel better.'
- 'I wish my mum would be less overprotective.'

What do you think is the hardest thing about being your age?

- 'Probably saying and doing stuff I don't mean because I feel annoyed, and then regretting it when I feel calmer.'
- 'That people expect us to act like adults – but when we do act like adults, we get treated like children.'
- 'Having to go through puberty.'
- 'Pressure from social media and the portrayal of perfection. Body-image pressures, even though I'm twelve.'
- 'Friendship problems.'
- 'No one listens to you.'
- 'Not being able to do what I want and being told "No" loads of times. I'd like to make my own decisions.'
- 'People assume that I know what they mean or want, but I don't always.'
- 'Your parents don't help you as much because they want you to be independent.'

- 'The fact there are stereotypes for the way we are meant to look and be.'
- 'How much work school expect of me.'
- 'Starting secondary school.'

What do you think is the best thing about being your age?

- 'Being able to play.'
- 'Being able to do stuff that I wasn't allowed to do when I was younger, like going on a rollercoaster or sitting shotgun in the front seat!'
- 'The freedom. I've never had very strict parents, but I like being able to get the bus with my friends and going shopping and helping my family.'
- 'I get whole new experiences when I move to. a new school.'
- 'Not having responsibilities or stress.'
- 'More grown-up chat and more thought-provoking discussions.'
- 'I get to go to the shop on my own.'
- 'That I get to do a lot of stuff on my own and that I understand lots.'
- 'I'm still young enough to go trick-or-treating.'
- 'You get more excited when it's your birthday or Christmas.'
- 'Learning new things every day.'
- 'Being with my family.'
- 'Knowing that people trust me to do more responsible things.'

I hope that this chapter has helped you to understand the mind of your tween a little more and given you some insight into the kind of parent or carer they need. Of course, I'm also aware of how hard it is to be a parent and I certainly don't want to leave you feeling worried that you somehow won't be able to measure up. None of us is perfect and it is unrealistic to aim to be so. Instead, I hope you will use the information in this chapter in the spirit in which it is intended – as a goal to slowly work towards over time (allowing for plenty of natural setbacks and mess-ups along the way), and not as a tick list or judgement of your parenting capabilities. Chapter 13 will look at your own emotions and behaviours a little more, but for now, let's move on to the next chapter, returning the focus to your tween's behaviour and how to cope with it.

Chapter 3

Typical Tween Behaviour – and How to Cope With It

'Behavior is what a man does, not what he thinks, feels or believes.'

EMILY DICKINSON, American poet

The above words, written by nineteenth-century American poet Emily Dickinson, epitomise my approach to dealing with all behaviour problems, whatever the age of the child (or indeed, adult).

Tween behaviour can stump many parents; gone is their sweet and co-operative little child and in their place is a stroppy, unco-operative backchatter. The most oft-given advice – to ignore or punish the bad behaviour and reward and praise the good – becomes less and less effective as children get older and can also make challenging behaviour worse. But why? Because these methods all presume that the underlying cause behind difficult behaviour is motivation. It isn't.

Motivation-based discipline methods – either those that aim to demotivate a specific tricky behaviour with the use of something that makes the child feel bad, such as punishment, shaming or exclusion; or those that aim to motivate a specific 'good' behaviour with the use of something that makes the child feel good, such as a reward or praise – will only work if there are no underlying problems at work. Most tweens are already motivated to behave in socially acceptable ways – just like us, they all want to feel good and don't enjoy the feelings that punishment and exclusion bring. But the reason why so many tweens behave in ways we don't appreciate has nothing to do with motivation, and everything to do with their neurological development and the environments and situations they find themselves in.

What does this mean for parents dealing with tween behaviour? An element of acceptance is always needed, by which I mean understanding what your tween is capable of and not expecting more of them. Just as we would not expect a three-month-old baby to walk, and we accept this natural developmental limitation, we should not expect a tween to behave with the full maturity of an adult. Understanding and accepting the neurological limitations of children is so important. By expecting too much of them we set them – and ourselves – up for failure. But does this mean we should never attempt to discipline, or to change any of the challenging behaviours our tweens demonstrate? Should we just 'suck it up'? No. There are ways to tweak behaviour gently and effectively; and most importantly, the best answer to any behaviour problem is to uncover and remedy its root cause. This chapter will concentrate on these things.

What is the best way to discipline tweens?

I use the acronym ACCLAIM – a word meaning appreciation and celebration – to summarise the best ways to approach any tween behaviour problems:

- Authoritative
- Collaborative
- Conscious
- Loving
- Aware
- Investigative
- Mindful

Let's look at the meanings of these words, and how they apply to tween discipline.

Authoritative

As we have already seen in the previous chapter, the most successful parenting style is one that is authoritative, not permissive, dismissive or authoritarian. This means approaching any behaviour issues with the key facets of authoritative parenting: realistic expectations of behaviour and an understanding of neurological capabilities; a good balance of control between parent or carer and child; and a high level of nurturance with the parent or carer in the role of the child's champion.

Collaborative

The best way to solve the problems underlying difficult behaviour is to work together with your tween. So many parents and carers create a gulf between themselves and their tweens with their attempts at discipline, and this disconnect only serves to make behaviour worse. The most effective solutions happen when a team works well together: collaboratively, with a strong connection. And the same is true of working with our tweens. So rather than asking, 'How do I get my tween to do ... ?' change your thinking to, 'How can my tween and I work together to solve this problem?'

Conscious

Raising tweens can be incredibly triggering for parents and carers, especially when they behave in ways that we ourselves would have been severely punished or admonished for at the same age. Our first response may be to react in the same ways we were disciplined as children, usually with anger. However, this serves only to perpetuate the cycle, doing nothing to solve its causes, and it certainly doesn't help tweens learn how to behave better next time. We must parent consciously – with an awareness of the triggers and feelings within us – and take a breath before we respond. Ask yourself, 'Why do I feel the need to respond to this? Is it because I am consciously bothered? Or is it because I would have been told off for this behaviour at the same age?'

Loving

When tweens feel supported and heard by their parents and carers, their behaviour is naturally better. When they feel they have somebody they can be their authentic selves with – someone who will listen without judgement and provide potential solutions – they are much more likely to confess their worries and concerns. This is the step that so many, including myself, find the hardest; when children are acting in horrible ways, saying hurtful things, it can be so hard to dig deep and find the grace to respond with love and understanding. But it is the only way that works. As American writer and humorist Erma Bombeck said, 'Kids need love the most when they're acting most unlovable.'

Aware

Being aware of your own feelings and actions as a parent or carer is a natural follow-on from the 'loving' point above. Being aware means understanding the impact you have as a role model and acknowledging that anything that you say or do will be teaching your tween. Do you always behave in ways that you would be happy with your tween mimicking? Very often, the behaviours we find the most challenging are ones that our tweens are reflecting back at us – holding up a mirror to our own anger, impatience or rudeness. I am regularly asked how to change a tween's behaviour, and parents and carers are usually surprised when I reply that the easiest way is to change their own behaviour first. All too frequently, we try to change our children with no recognition that things would be a lot easier for us if we changed ourselves and our own actions, too.

Being aware of your own behaviours and expectations also means sometimes letting behaviour slide. You don't need to discipline everything, and you don't need to respond to every tricky behaviour your tween displays or to every triggering word that they say. It's OK to be selective. Commonly, this is referred to as 'picking your battles', but I personally hate this phrase. It implies that raising children is combative, when it should be collaborative, so I much prefer to say, 'Let it slide.'

Investigative

I often think that the role of parent or carer to tweens needs similar skills to that of a detective. Think of yourself as the Hercule Poirot or Sherlock Holmes of eight- to thirteen-year-olds. You constantly need to ask yourself, 'Why?' Why is my tween acting in this way? Why are they feeling like this? Why are they not responding to me in ways I would like? Why are they finding what is expected of them so difficult? Investigating the underlying causes of behaviour is so important, yet so rarely done.

Mindful

While we should have an awareness of our own feelings, we must also be aware – or mindful – of those of our tweens, too. In psychology, the term 'mind-minded parenting' means accepting that all children (even babies) have their own independent thoughts and feelings. When we are mindful of this, we approach behaviour problems in a way that automatically makes any solution collaborative.

Responding to behaviour – short term versus long term

Many attempts at disciplining tweens fail because they are approached only with a short-term 'fix-it' mentality. However, we must consider and resolve the causes of the behaviour in order to encourage a deep, long-term change, as well as looking at how to respond 'in the moment', or the short term. For instance, if a tween is being violent, we need to stop the hitting in the short term – but then we must also look for the cause of the dysregulation. We must ask why the tween was feeling so bad that they ended up needing to hit in the first place. If we don't, the behaviour will continue and even escalate, no matter how we deal with it in the moment. This blend of short-term (in the moment) and long-term (finding the why) discipline is essential if we really want to extinguish specific tricky behaviours.

In addition to considering short- and long-term solutions,

we must also think about how we, as adults, are acting and what sort of role models we are. This is where Bion's idea of containment comes in, too (see page 50). Are we being effect-ive containers for our tweens? Or do we need time for some introspection to make sure that we are better role models and containers? I like to think of this three-pronged approach to discipline – considering the short term, the long term and the impact of ourselves – as a tree. We are the trunk, the secure base of the tree (providing containment, roots, stability and role modelling), with short-term discipline as a branch to the left and long-term discipline as a branch to the right. We need to consider all three for our attempts to be successful. Interestingly, this tree looks remarkably like psi, the twenty-third letter of the Greek alphabet:

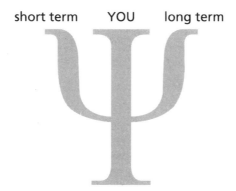

Psi is commonly used by psychologists as an abbreviation for the word psychology, but I find it helpful to remember the image of the psi symbol and the two-branched tree when trying to decipher how to respond to tricky tween behaviour. For me, it is the perfect symbol of tween psychology or parenting, and we will apply this approach to some of the most common tricky tween behaviours for the remainder of this chapter.

Backchat and rudeness

Answering back, often known as backchat (things like, 'Why should I?', 'No! I'm not doing it', 'I don't want to!' and 'I hate you, you're so mean!'), arguing when you ask them to do something and rudeness often top the list of tween behaviours that parents and carers have issues with.

Short-term considerations

- Could you 'let it slide'? Remember you don't need to respond to everything.
- Respond to the emotion, not the words. You could say, 'I hear that you're upset with that request. What can we do to make it easier for you?'
- Take a moment to focus fully on your child. Backchat is often a bid for your attention (even negative attention is attention for a tween) and is a sure-fire way to grab it. Try saying, 'OK, I'm listening. What's up? How can I help?'

Long-term considerations

- Ask yourself if what you are asking your tween to do is truly age-appropriate and fair to them. Can you tweak your request to make it easier for them to comply?
- If you feel that your tween's backchat is caused, at least in part, by their need for more attention from you, work out a way to spend more one-to-one time with them, to work on your connection.
- Is the backchat triggered by something else that your tween is going through? Do they have any difficult or big feelings they are currently struggling with and your request has been the final straw, causing them to bubble

over? How can you help them to offload and make some space?

Considering your own impact

- Have you been clear enough with your communication? Does your tween fully understand what is expected from them, including time frames? Confusion and misunderstanding can often trigger a challenging response.
- Are you being triggered? Is your tween responding in a way that you would have been admonished or punished for at their age? Remember: you are not your parents and you don't need to respond in the same way that they did.
- Don't join in on their dysregulation. Mirror back calm, not anger. Take a deep breath and consider the sort of behaviour you are modelling to your tween when it comes to handling difficult interactions with others. How would you feel in their position?
- Do you need to be more consistent with upholding your boundaries; or alternatively, more flexible? A lot of back-chat is a natural pushback to rules and expectations. It is the tween's role to do this, to find their place in the world, and it is your role to carefully choose boundaries and be consistent with them.
- Are you being respectful in your communication? Ask yourself how you would feel if you were spoken to in the way that you have spoken to them. Would you feel respected and valued (and more likely to respond positively)?

Deliberately breaking rules

Have you heard the saying 'rules are made to be broken'? This couldn't be more apt in the tween years. Part of the job of a tween is to break away from their parents and carers and forge their own path in life. To do this, they must be a little selfish and focus on their own needs and wants more than those of others. They need to test your boundaries and push back against rules that are set – not because they are being deliberately naughty, but because they need to develop an awareness of who they are in the world and what they can and can't do in this new role.

Short-term considerations

- Could you 'let it slide'? What's the worst that would happen if you didn't uphold your rule or you changed it?
- Does your tween understand the repercussions and need for the rule? Very often, tweens ignore and challenge rules because they don't fully understand their value. Taking a moment to explain why the rule exists, what could happen if it didn't and how it ultimately helps to keep everybody safe and happy can have a huge positive impact on compliance. Of course, it's also OK for you to change your mind and relax or remove the rule if, during this process, the questioning leads you to reassess its importance.
- Can you come to a collaborative solution? Ask your tween how they think the rule could be tweaked to keep you both happy.

Long-term considerations

- Are your rules age-appropriate? Are you expecting your tween to behave older than their years? Alternatively, do you need to relax or change your rules as your tween gets older, giving them more autonomy?
- Do you have too many rules? Is it hard for your tween to stick to them because of this? Giving them a little freedom in the areas that matter least can really help them to stick to the big 'deal-breaker' rules.
- Do you show your tween enough trust or give them opportunities to gain it? Sometimes rules can make tweens feel you don't trust them, and giving them chances to show you that they are worthy of more trust as they get a little older can be very productive.
- Are there other reasons they are having problems with a particular rule? Peer pressure, perhaps, or teasing from friends? Often, it isn't the rule at all, but something else in their life that is making it hard for them to stick to it.

Considering your own impact

- Are your rules mindfully set? Ask yourself why you have them? Is it because you were set the same ones as a tween, because your friends set them for their children, because you've read something online or because you genuinely believe they are important? Only the latter is a genuine reason for setting any rule.
- Do you consistently reinforce your rules? If you sometimes ignore them, you are telling your tween that it is always worth challenging you because this could be the time that you let a rule slip. If a rule is important to you, you must always uphold it, no matter the situation.

- Do you follow your own rules? There is nothing more damaging to your tween's respect for you than watching you break the very rules that you have set for them. If a rule matters to you, then you should observe it, too. If you have a rule over screen-time usage, your tween is not going to respect it if you are constantly on your phone yourself. Remember, you are their role model!
- Do you respond maturely in a way that helps your tween to understand the importance of the rules and your position? Calmly and rationally explaining your position is the only way to get a tween to genuinely respect and, ultimately, follow a rule.

Sulking

Do you remember sulking as a tween? Sulking was my 'go-to' response to anything that I didn't like for many years. I used to storm up to my room, banging the door loudly for added drama, and then I would throw myself onto my bed, alternating between sighing, crying and scowling. I remember vividly what I really wanted – or should I say, needed – at the time: for my parents to come and check on me and help make things right; I wanted them to listen to me and give me some attention in the form of a big, warm hug. I didn't necessarily want to always be right or get my own way. I just needed them to see me and my feelings.

Short-term considerations

- Parents are commonly advised to completely ignore sulking to show tweens that they won't get their own way with their dramatic behaviour. I hope my example of my own memory, above, and perhaps your own show

how incorrect this advice is. A sulking tween is one who desperately needs connection with their carers.

- While your tween does need connection with you, it doesn't mean that you should allow them to get their own way. You can uphold your boundary and still make them feel seen and heard. Saying, 'I can see you're really upset; how can we make this work for both of us?' is still authoritative.
- Finally, about connection: some tweens do genuinely need their own space before reconnecting with you. The key here is to follow your tween's lead. If they need time on their own, respect this, but make sure they know you are there if and when they are ready.

Long-term considerations

- Sulking commonly occurs when tweens are feeling disconnected from their parents and feel a lack of understanding and empathy from them. Spending some time with your tween when they are calm, discussing how to help them when they get overwhelmed with big emotions, can be extremely helpful, as can increasing the time you spend with them one to one, enjoying each other's company.
- Sulking also happens when tweens feel a lack of control over their own lives. Encouraging your tween to contribute to house rules and allowing them to make choices, where appropriate, to show that you trust and value their growing maturity can be helpful.

Considering your own impact

- Sulking can be so hard to deal with as a parent, commonly because it triggers us to respond in the way we were responded to when we sulked as tweens. Many of us were raised with the view that sulking was an incredibly negative behaviour that should be ignored or punished. Remember, you can break this cycle. You don't have to treat your child in the same way as you were treated.

- Remember also that your child will mirror your actions. Now is very much a time to 'be the adult'. Don't join your tween by having your own sulk.

Swearing and cursing

For many parents and carers, overhearing their tween swearing and cursing or, indeed, being on the receiving end of rude words, can make them see red. Very quickly, the situation can escalate into something far more damaging and serious if you do not take mindful action.

Short-term considerations

- Try to 'let it slide', if you can. Aim to ignore the actual words spoken, responding instead to the feelings behind them. For instance, if your tween is swearing when they are clearly angry, you could say, 'I can hear you are very angry. Tell me more about how you're feeling.'
- Explain to your tween why the words they are using are inappropriate and potentially hurtful. Recognise that they need to express themselves but give them alternative and acceptable words to use instead. Ensure they know that you do not appreciate certain words being directed at you or spoken when they are in public.

Long-term considerations

- Tweens have little self-control, and although many know that swearing is unacceptable, it can be hard to control the impulse in the moment. Helping tweens to understand their own brain development can work well here, as it allows them to realise that their struggles with things such as impulse control and emotion regulation are not personality flaws or failings, but a normal stage of development that all tweens go through. Likewise, teaching them other coping mechanisms and alternative words to use when they feel the need to swear can be useful.
- Once again, if your tween is swearing when in a heightened state of emotion, then looking for causes of the big emotions that ultimately lead to swearing is key. What is it that has triggered your tween so much? Can you help them to resolve the problem?
- Be aware of what your tween is being exposed to – computer games or television programmes, for example – and decide whether they are age-appropriate.

Considering your own impact

- Tweens often learn to swear from us, their parents and carers, just as they learn other vocabulary organically from us. If we swear at home, we will raise children who do the same, regardless of whether we tell them that they shouldn't. Role-model the vocabulary you want your tween to use, not that which you don't. This applies for all adults your tween spends time with, which may mean you need to have a conversation with the other adults in their life.

'I hate you!'

After several years of hearing your cute toddler, preschooler and infant-school-aged child profess their undying love for you, it can come as a shock the first time your tween announces that they hate you. Sometimes their actions, and especially their words, can seem like a bullet to your heart. Take solace in the fact that this isn't uncommon and really doesn't indicate that your tween no longer loves you.

Short-term considerations

- Once again, focus on the emotions and not the words. What your tween is really saying is, 'I'm really angry with you and I'm finding it so hard to love you right at this moment.' As an adult, you have the vocabulary and the emotional literacy to phrase these feelings correctly; your tween doesn't. Don't react to the 'I-don't-love-you' sentiment. Instead, respond to the underlying emotions.
- When you reply, stay calm and gently say, 'I can hear that you're angry with me now, and that's OK. I understand. I will always love you and I'm here if you need me to help you.'

Long-term considerations

- Now is the time for some investigative work. Sometimes the 'I hate yous' are an obvious response to a request you have made, such as asking your tween to do their homework or tidy their room. Other times, though, they cover up deeper worries and concerns. Can you decipher what has caused your tween to feel this way?

- Often, 'I hate you' illustrates that your tween is feeling a disconnect with you. This could be because you are pre-occupied with something or somebody else or because of spending more time physically away from each other. Trying to rebuild the connection will usually help.
- Tweens sometimes need to vent their frustrations at us. We are their safe place. When your tween gets angry and lashes out at you verbally, it may have nothing to do with you. They could have been storing up some difficult emotions arising from friendship issues or something that they are unhappy with at school. You just so happened to be in the firing range when they finally exploded. Again, working with your tween to identify and help them with the underlying cause is the ultimate solution.

Considering your own impact

- Once again, now is the time to be the adult. Try to see through the words that your tween is saying and understand that they are hurting. This is probably not about you at all. Take a deep breath, stay calm and remind yourself that you are the one with the adult brain. Don't react with a childlike response, no matter how hurt you may feel.
- To be the adult, you need to be kind to yourself. Again, don't dwell on the words themselves or convince yourself that your tween hates you. They don't. They just hate the situation they are in or the emotions they are feeling. Remind yourself that you are a good parent and that your tween feels comfortable showing these big emotions to you because you have made them feel safe and secure enough to do so.

Messy rooms

Can you remember what your bedroom was like as a tween? My instinctive nature is to be messy. Conversely, however, I also like the spaces I live in to be clean and tidy. This dichotomy is one that frequently annoys me as an adult and used to drive my parents to distraction when I was a tween and teen. My room was either terribly untidy or spotless. Never anything in the middle. Even now, I veer between the two and, as you may expect, my children have grown to be just like me – something I'm not proud of, but totally understand. Messy rooms can be a constant source of frustration for parents and carers, but they don't need to be a frequent cause of arguments, too.

Short-term considerations

- This is a classic could you 'let-it-slide' situation. Ask yourself, 'What's the worst that will happen if their room is messy?'
- Come to a collaborative solution with your child. Is there anything that could help them to tidy? Facing a messy room is a daunting task at any age, but especially for tweens who don't yet have adult logical-thinking skills. Break down the task into smaller bite-size chunks – for example, 'OK, job number one: any rubbish is to go into this bag.' Then, 'When the rubbish is done, we need to pick up any dirty clothes and put them into the linen basket.' With simple, step-by-step instructions the task at hand becomes far less daunting and is much more likely to be completed.
- Work together to tidy the room and try to make it fun. Put on some loud music, sing along together or make up your own silly tidying-up song. Set yourself a time

to beat for getting the room complete. If you beat the time, choose a reward for working hard as a team, such as watching a movie together.

Long-term considerations

- Tweens don't think like us. We know if rooms are messy that things get accidentally broken. We know if carpets aren't hoovered or surfaces dusted that they are unhygienic. Tweens don't appreciate this unless it is broken down for them to understand. You could show your tween some pictures of dust mites or mould and explain that these are living in their room and that's why they need to tidy and hoover.
- Consider facilitating your tween's success. Help them to thin out their belongings so that they have less to clear up and help them with storage solutions that make it easier to keep things tidy. For instance, my own children struggled with putting clothes on hangers as tweens, so we ditched the wardrobes and used large chests of drawers instead, making putting their clothes away easier.

Considering your own impact

- Consider what you are role-modelling. Too many parents expect their children to keep their rooms tidy, when their own is messy. If you are messy, you will raise messy children. Don't expect them to be better than you. Think about reinventing the way tidying happens across your entire home, so that you all cope better.
- Learn to respect that your tween's space is their space, not yours. Although their mess may trigger you, it is their mess, in their room. And while that room may be in your home, it's important for tweens to have a sense

of autonomy and ownership. You may find it easier to work on them keeping the rest of the home tidy, while allowing them to do what they want in their own space. The state of their bedroom is not somehow a reflection of you or your parenting.

'I want, I want, I want . . . '

We live in an increasingly consumer society. Tweens today are bombarded with adverts wherever they are, both in the real world and in the virtual one, online. They are subjected to so much more advertising than we ever were at the same age. Even as recently as five years ago, the idea of 'unboxing' videos on social media was unheard of; now, hundreds of tweens and teens earn huge amounts of money simply recording them-selves unboxing the latest toys, trainers or confectionery. It is no surprise, then, that many tweens are always asking for more and more from their parents: toys, clothes, tech and anything else their favourite influencer, musician or actor is being paid to promote.

Short-term considerations

- Empathise with your tween's disappointment. Say, 'Wow, I wish I could have everything I wanted. It would be great if we had a magic wand or a genie to grant our every wish. What would you wish for first?'
- After reiterating that it is not possible to buy what-ever your tween wants, when they want it, you could encourage them to choose something in particular (note – not everything), so that they can add it to a Christmas or birthday list, or make it something to save towards. This list is often quite fickle, and many things

drop off it before the money is saved or a special event comes around.

Long-term considerations

- Carefully consider what your tween is being exposed to. Unboxing videos can seem like harmless fun, but it is cleverly designed to encourage children to want what is being unboxed.
- Introducing pocket money is perhaps the best way to tackle this issue. If children have financial freedom and the means to purchase what they want (albeit not always when they want it), the 'I-want-this' requests lessen dramatically. (We will look at pocket money and how to approach it in Chapter 12.)
- Sometimes the requests to buy items signal an attempt from your tween to fit in with their peers. This can indicate potential friendship and self-esteem issues, so do dig a little deeper to find out why your child is so desperate for something; it may not be about the specific item they are requesting at all.

Considering your own impact

- What sort of a relationship do you have with consumerism? Are you the first one to queue when the January sales or Black Friday start? What message are you giving your child about purchasing and desiring objects? Thinning out your own belongings and focusing on a more minimalist home can really help here. Also, look at the number of gifts you buy your child and when. Are you somehow showing them that buying or receiving equate to feeling good or resolving difficult emotions?

Lying

Can you remember a time from your tween years when you lied to your parent or carer, or even a teacher? What motivated you to lie? We often view lying as despicable behaviour in children; however, we are frequently blind to the fact that most lying comes from a good place or one of self-preservation: to save somebody's feelings, to avoid letting them down or to avoid getting into trouble for fear of what might happen if they tell the truth. None of these reasons is nasty or spiteful, yet, all too often, adults treat lying as if it is one of the worst behaviours their tween could exhibit.

Short-term considerations

- If you want your tween to tell you the truth, you must make sure they are not scared to do so. This means staying calm and avoiding harsh punishments, no matter how hard it is for you to hear that truth.
- Tell your tween that they can always be honest with you; you will always try to understand and help them, no matter what they have done. Explain that you may sometimes be angry initially, but that you will always value them telling the truth.

Long-term considerations

- Help your tween to feel safe telling you anything. This doesn't just include things they have done but also things others have done (and maybe done to them). This comes back once again to the idea of containment and metaphorically holding their truth – making space to hear it and help with any repercussions.

- Working on your relationship with your tween is key. The more respected they feel by you and the more you treat them fairly and empathetically, the more likely they are to tell you the truth. Fostering open and honest communication is the goal.

Considering your own impact

- Think about the reasons why you lie and how often you do it. When did you last tell somebody you loved their haircut when you really disliked it, or gave an excuse for being late that was entirely made up? Remember, our tweens are watching us. The more we lie, for whatever reason, the more we model to them that lying is an acceptable and, indeed, desirable social skill.
- Controlling your reaction to your tween's truth is probably the biggest deciding factor in whether they feel able to be honest with you the next time they do something that you disagree with. No matter how let down or angry you feel with them, remember, your reaction is everything. Try to stay calm and let them know that above all else, you value them telling you the truth.

Sibling squabbles

For those who have brothers and sisters, fights and fallings-out with siblings are a mainstay of childhood. I am often asked how to solve sibling rivalry, and my honest opinion is that you can't and, indeed, you shouldn't want to either. Sibling squabbles are a great introduction to dealing with relationship complications and negotiating solutions – a wonderful skill for later in life. Too often, television shows or books portray Waltonesque families, where the children are all best friends with each other. This simply isn't realistic. Yes, some siblings do have wonderful relationships and rarely fall out, but many more bicker seemingly constantly through their tween years. This categorically is not an indicator of what their future relationships will be like and is certainly not a reflection of your parenting skills.

Short-term considerations

- The more my children bickered with each other, the more I learned that it was better for me to be involved as little as possible. Each time I intervened, I took away a chance for them to reach a solution without me. Keeping your intervention to a minimum is the quickest way for them to navigate this phase.
- When you do need to intervene (for me, anything involving safety was a deal-breaker for allowing them to resolve things independently), try to adopt the role of a referee rather than a judge. Instead of giving an order and taking a side, say, 'I can see you're both angry. I would like to hear what you both have to say, one by one, and then I would like to hear how you think you can solve this problem.'

Long-term considerations

- A lot of sibling rivalry stems from a feeling that parents are favouring one child over another. This can be based on material goods, but children are often more concerned about attention. The solution here is to give each sibling as much one-to-one time with you as possible. I am a huge advocate of trying to spend a whole day with one child on their own, away from any siblings – once a month, if possible – but certainly no less frequently than every six months. Use this time to reconnect with each other and make the child feel like they are the centre of your world again.

- Help your children to respect each other's space by giving them clearly defined personal spaces. This doesn't necessarily have to be their own rooms. It could be a cupboard that is sacred to them and is not allowed to be touched by anybody without their permission. Don't force them to share (either their space or their belongings); you can encourage it, but respect their decision if they don't want to.

- Be really careful not to label your children. For instance, 'Oh, he's the difficult one', or, 'She's so much easier than her sister.' Children pick up on these comments and take them to heart, often acting out the roles they have been assigned.

Considering your own impact

- If your children are squabbling, ask yourself why you feel the need to intervene? If they are not hurting each other or damaging belongings, what can you do to enable yourself to sit on your hands and allow them the opportunity to resolve their disagreement independently?

- Be careful not to relive your relationship with your own siblings through your children. They are not you or your siblings just as you are not your parents. You do not have to treat them in the same way.

- Be mindful of how you speak to your children. Notice your tone. Do you tend to be harsher to one than the other, perhaps because of age or size differences? Children are incredibly perceptive; they will pick up on these conscious (and often unconscious) biases and it absolutely can impact their relationships with their siblings.

While this chapter is by no means an exhaustive list of tween behaviour issues and ways to approach them, I hope that it has given you some insight into how to respond to tweens in an authoritative, effective and collaborative way. Remembering the psi symbol or the tree with two branches (short term and long term) with you in the middle will help you to approach any issue in a holistic way. It is, indeed, the only way to produce long-term, positive results.

For the remainder of this book, we will take a closer look at some of the most pertinent issues facing tweens and their parents and carers today, starting with a look at friendship issues in the next chapter.

Chapter 4

Friends, Foes and Frenemies

'You have been my best friend,' replied Charlotte.
'That in itself is a tremendous thing.'
Charlotte's Web, E. B. White

Tweens' relationships, both with parents and carers and with friends, play a key role in their current and future happiness. So far in this book, we have focused on your tween's relationship with you. A sense of acceptance and belonging with you is an important foundation in Maslow's pyramid (see page 49), but this also needs to happen with their peers. Good friendships can help tweens through many tricky times and transitions. Research has found that having just one close and supportive friend in childhood increases resilience and coping skills.[1] Strong friendships can also help tweens academically and emotionally and shape their relationships (including romantic) later in life, but if they have problems with friendships, the world can feel like an unwelcoming and challenging place.

Research has shown that tweens today are becoming increasingly unhappy with their friendships, with over 5 per cent reporting extreme friendship worries.[2] While friendships in the early years of childhood are relatively simple and straightforward, as children approach the tween years, they can become fraught with tension, with constant fallings-out, bickering, exclusion, peer pressure, the development of cliques and bullying. This can understandably have a huge impact on tween wellbeing.

So if your tween is having a hard time with their peer relationships, how can you help them? In this chapter, we will cover the most common issues and consider how to raise a tween who is equipped to navigate the choppy waters that characterise friendships between eight- to thirteen-year-olds.

Self-esteem

You may be wondering why I would start a chapter on friendships with self-esteem. Well, the relationships we have with others are all underpinned by the relationship we have with ourselves. Tweens who are happy in their own skins, confident and who have an appreciation of their own worth are more likely to form fulfilling friendships. Conversely, those who struggle with self-esteem can fall into toxic friendships, which further damage their confidence, or they may find it harder to make friends in the first place. Whatever friendship worries your tween may be having, helping them to like themselves is a sensible starting point.

The following tips can all help to increase self-esteem in tweens:

- Teach your tween to focus on the things they like best about themselves, both physically and personality-wise. You could work together on a list of 'reasons why I like myself', encouraging them to pinpoint their best traits and why they make a great friend.

- Following on from the previous point, help your tween to be aware of their own negative self-talk. Each time they think something bad about themselves, encourage them to stop the train of thought and ask themselves why they think this and if the thought is helping or hurting them. If it is hurtful, encourage them to focus on something good about themselves instead.

- Look for a hobby that your tween really enjoys. It doesn't have to be one where they meet other people, or make friends; this is all about giving them something that really interests them and helps them to occupy their time in a way that is fulfilling for them.

- Learn mindfulness with your tween. Mindfulness means focusing on the present moment and appreciating it, instead of letting your mind run ahead with anxiety about the future or concerns about the past. A common form of mindfulness involves simple breathing techniques, some of which we will cover in the next chapter (see page 122). You could also introduce the idea of positive affirmations. These are simple, positive statements that your tween can speak aloud, listen to on a recording, write out or display on pre-made cards around their room. Again, this is covered in more detail in the next chapter (see page 123).

- Try to set up situations where your tween will succeed. For instance, if they are gifted physically, you could encourage them to join a local sports club.

- When you do praise your tween, focus on the effort they have put in, not the outcome. So if they have done particularly well at a piece of school work, don't say, 'You're so clever, well done!' Instead, say, 'I'm so proud of all the work you put into this piece of homework. I watched you try really hard at it.' If you focus on the outcome too much, you run the risk of causing your tween to be anxious about always succeeding, which can undermine their self-esteem. Effort-based praise, on the other hand, acknowledges the work they put in, regardless of how well they do at the final task. You want them to feel proud of themselves for trying, not focusing entirely on the outcome.

- Teach your tween gratitude and kindness. When we are stressed, we secrete hormones that send us into the fight-or-flight response. These hormones make us feel anxious and uncomfortable, both physically and emotionally. When we focus on gratitude and kindness (to ourselves and others) we secrete hormones that make us feel happy and calm. You could encourage your tween to come up with some 'random acts of kindness' – leaving a book on a park bench with a 'please-take-me-home-and-read-me' label, or picking some flowers from your garden to give to an elderly neighbour. These acts will help your tween to secrete lots of happy hormones and allow them to feel better about themselves (as well as improving the lives of those on the receiving end of their kindness).

- Show your tween how to respect themselves by giving them respect. This is such a simple concept, but one so often missed in much parenting advice. The more you respect your tween, the more they will feel worthy of respect from others and themselves. Let them know that their opinions matter to you – actively listen to their concerns with empathy.

Self-esteem is a work in progress. Sadly, there is no one trick that will boost it overnight. However, just a little bit of effort each day really can make a big difference over time.

Introversion and extroversion in the tween years

Do you consider yourself an introvert or an extrovert? I firmly identify in the introvert camp and I spent most of my tween and teen years thinking there was something wrong with me. My parents were both extroverts, as were all my friends. I don't think any of them fully understood me as a child. I distinctly remember my social-butterfly mother desperately trying to stop me being so shy – she was worried that I didn't have many friends and was often alone. Shy became a word that I associated with myself. I believed it was a personality flaw, and the more I focused on trying not to be so shy, the more I retreated into my shell. Now, as an adult, I no longer identify with the word shy. I know I'm an introvert and I don't consider it something negative, but it took me a long time to understand and make peace with this.

As a child, I always preferred spending time with only one close friend, rather than a group. I thrived on my own, loved being at home and after spending any length of time in a group of people I felt a desperate need to retreat and be alone again. Alone time charged my batteries; time with lots of others depleted them. I liked silence and solitude. I didn't enjoy meeting new people or making new friends. I still don't, and my closest friends remain those I've had since high school. None of this is shyness or problematic behaviour for a natural introvert, and therefore there is no need for parents to be worried.

Related to the concept of introversion and extroversion is that of leaders and followers in friendships. Leaders tend to be extroverted, skilled communicators, whereas followers tend to be more introverted and quieter. Parents may worry if their child always seems to take the follower role in a friendship, believing that this is somehow a negative pattern for their tween – but it's

OK to be either, so long as the child is happy. The balance of control in friendships tends to even out as children grow, with more democratic groups forming at secondary school, as older teens become better able to assess the values of different alliances and the way people, including themselves, are treated.

Worried parents often ask me how they can encourage introverted tweens to be more sociable and to join in with other children, but, in my experience, this anxiety tends to be unfounded and says more about the parents' concerns and feelings than those of their children. Parents should try hard not to transfer their own feelings onto their tweens. I tend to find those who struggle the most are parents who are naturally very extroverted – the life and soul of the party, with a wide circle of friends – and are raising a naturally introverted child who prefers solitude, or spending time with just one close friend. The key is asking yourself if your tween is happy alone: if they are, then accepting their introversion is the best way forward; if they aren't, then helping them to make more friends is the way to go. But it's not only introverts who may need help with making (and keeping) friends – sometimes extroverts can have a hard time, too.

Making friends

Watching your child stand alone in a playground, surrounded by groups of children seemingly happily chatting together, is one of the most heartbreaking experiences for a parent. Most of my children made friends easily, but one had real difficulties in his tween years. He was a lovely, kind, quiet boy, but he didn't like the sports that other boys in his year were into, and when they all dashed off to play football at lunchtime, he would often be left sitting on a bench alone. The lack of common ground made it hard for him to connect with others and for a year or so at primary school he really found friendships challenging. Things changed when he moved to secondary school – with so many more children, he found it easier to meet kindred spirits.

The following ideas can all help if you find yourself in a similar position with your tween:

- Encourage your tween to find common ground with others – for instance, a shared love of music or a particular sporting activity or team.
- Talk to your tween about introductions and how to break the ice. You might suggest they smile and introduce themselves and ask the other child's name, rather than waiting for the other child to do it first. If the other child is an introvert, it's highly unlikely that will happen!
- Help your tween with conversation starters. Encourage them to ask questions about what the other child enjoys doing. Suggest a few stock questions, such as, 'What's your favourite television programme?' 'What music do you like?' 'What's your best, or worst, subject?' Make sure to keep the questions open-ended, to avoid conversation-ending 'Yes' or 'No' answers.
- Suggest that they compliment other tweens who they would like to strike up a friendship with. They could say, 'I really like your shoes' or, 'Your bag is really cool!'
- Help your tween to listen carefully to others, show interest in what is being said and know when it's important to be quiet and give the other child time to speak.
- If there is another child yours particularly gravitates towards, suggest that it could be a nice idea to invite them round to your home. If you know the other child's parents, you could approach them directly if your own child is worried about asking.
- Teach your child how to be assertive (but not aggressive) if somebody says or does something that they don't

like. Explain the difference between assertiveness and coming across as impolite or unfriendly, so scaring away potential friends.

As well as discussions with your tween, do have a chat with their class teacher or form tutor if problems occur at school. Staff are very experienced at working with friendship issues and they may have extra ideas or schemes that can be put into place at school for your tween.

Cliques, social exclusion and toxic friendships

Friendships in the early years tend to be simple and straightforward. Young children usually make up as quickly and easily as they fall out and rarely require much adult intervention to repair any friendship ruptures. But as children enter their last years in primary school, a shift often occurs, with groups forming that exclude other tweens, and friendships sometimes taking on more toxic elements. I am a huge critic of gender stereotyping children, but this is one area that does tend to be quite different for boys and girls, with the formation of cliques being far more common among girls.

When my first three children – all boys – were at primary school, I would often hear comments from girls' mums about friendship issues and find it hard to identify with. When my youngest, a girl, reached her tween years, I finally understood. Her last two years of primary school were full of drama and tears because of the changing friendships among the girls – so much so that I found it hard to keep up to date with what was happening and often felt at a loss when my daughter came home in tears because of some disagreement, exclusion or hurtful words. Of course, this isn't to say that boys don't have difficulties, too – they do – but more issues seem to occur with girls. I suppose I am biased here, being female, and somebody who attended an all-girls high school, but research does show that girls have more problems with friendships in the tween years than boys.[3]

One thing I have learned in my years of parenting is that you cannot choose your tween's friends, nor can you make them stop being friends with anyone. As frustrating as this is, especially if you are seeing them hurt over and over again by another, you will be wasting your breath with any attempt at breaking up the friendship, and you could well drive a wedge between you and your tween, leaving them feeling that they can no longer speak to you about these things. So if your tween is experiencing friendship issues, particularly involving social exclusion, cliques or toxic friendships (those appearing to cause more harm than good), don't try to split up a friendship. That said, this doesn't mean doing nothing; it just means you need to support your tween, while they come to their own conclusion that the friendship is not a positive one for them. Give the following tips a try:

- Help your tween to understand why their friend (or past friend) may be acting in the way they are. When children are mean to those they are (or were) friends with, it usually says more about them than the child on the receiving end. Helping tweens to understand this can really help to protect their self-esteem.
- Work on your tween's self-worth and help them to see that they are worthy of respect from their friends and don't deserve to be ill-treated. If tweens believe they are worth more, they expect more.
- Discuss the idea of being 'popular' with your tween (in the sense of tween social status). Talk about the fact that popularity doesn't automatically make you a nicer person, nor is it necessarily something to aspire to. A lot of popular people can be quite mean and, in this case,

their popularity usually doesn't last once their true colours are recognised.

- Encourage your tween not to get involved in gossip and rumours. The more they can avoid any potentially negative talk about others, the better – not only because it is unkind but also because conversations that tweens think are private with so-called friends often have a habit of not staying private.

- Ask teachers and other school staff if they have any insider information on what is happening and request that they unobtrusively monitor things and, potentially, organise a class discussion about gossip, social exclusion and friendship issues.

- Be there to listen and provide emotional support to your tween whenever needed and remember that if they are finding friendships challenging, their behaviour at home with you may become difficult.

- See if you can discreetly help your child to expand their circle of friends. You could, perhaps, arrange tea after school, sleepovers or weekend social gatherings with children they are already friendly with, but perhaps not as close to as those they are having problems with.

- Explain the idea of manipulation and gaslighting to your tween (gaslighting being a form of psychological control where an individual makes you feel as if something is all your fault and you are the problem, when, in fact, it is the other way around). Help your tween to spot when this control or manipulation may be happening to them.

- Discuss coping strategies for times when your tween may be alone, particularly at school. For instance, can they go into the library to read, or volunteer to help play with the younger children, if this is an option at their school.

- If your tween has access to a mobile phone or the internet, consider whether it would be better for them to go offline for a while; often, a lot of toxicity occurs in group chats and text messages.

Whatever your tween is facing with friendships, remember your role is to empower them, not to take over and try to fix things for them. While it may be tempting to try to swoop in and make everything better, you will be depriving them of vital inter-personal skills and they will struggle again the next time it happens. See your role as a guide and a coach, gently leading your tween towards independent problem solving. Finally, try not to be too judgemental – sometimes a friendship continues for many years, no matter how toxic you think it may be, and your tween may not come to you for advice in the future if you have expressed misgivings in the past.

Teaching tweens how to tackle issues with otherwise good friends

Even the most positive of friendships can run into trouble, and in the tween years, with all the changing brain development affecting social skills, it's unsurprising that most tweens grapple with friendships at times. The term 'frenemies' is often used to describe the seemingly fickle friendships at this age that alternate between being best friends and sworn enemies on an almost weekly basis. The fallings-out and making-ups can seem never-ending when you're raising a tween – so much so that you may wonder if there is a larger underlying problem. Rest assured that this is an incredibly common and normal pattern for this age group, and these friendship issues provide a great education in inter-personal skills and conflict resolution that will stand your tween in good stead for future relationships.

The following tips can help your tween if they have problems with otherwise good friends.

- Teach your tween how to apologise. Perhaps the best way to do this is to model a great apology when you do or say something you shouldn't have to your tween. If they see you regularly apologise, they are more likely to copy your behaviour if they have said or done something that upsets a friend.

- Encourage your tween to empathise with how their friend feels. The tween years are inherently egocentric, and many can find it hard to understand the viewpoints and emotions of others. They often focus so much on their own feelings and how wronged they feel in a friendship that they miss the other child's. Ask, 'How do you think your friend feels right now? Do you think they are feeling upset like you?' And, 'When you had the argument, can you imagine what it was like for your friend?'

- If the falling-out happens at school or at a club your tween regularly attends, encourage them to confide in trusted adults and ask for their help and advice if they cannot resolve things independently at the time.

- If your tween's attempts at apologising are in vain, help them to understand that sometimes we all need a little time and space away from those who hurt us. Just because their friend is not ready to make up yet, it doesn't mean that the rift will last for ever.

- Help your tween to communicate in ways that are more likely to be understood by their friend. Here you could teach them to use 'I' statements. These involve starting a conversation with 'I' rather than 'You'. For instance: 'I felt really sad when you said that', rather than negative statements about their friend such as, 'You're so mean!' I statements encourage positive communication because they are not accusatory, but they are not naturally used by tweens.

- Consider inviting their friend (with their parent, if you get along with them) out for the day to do something fun. This can take the pressure off the children, but the fun time together can often encourage a truce.

Changing friendships

The tween years are a time of tremendous change and friendships do not escape this transition. Sadly, some of the best friendships of early childhood come to an end as adolescence approaches, particularly as tweens start secondary school. Children all mature at different rates and, as they grow, it is common for interests to change, often resulting in friendships running their course. Tweens often start secondary school retaining one or more of their closest friendships from primary school (even if they attend different schools), but as the year progresses, you often find that they start to find more kindred spirits, with a much larger pool of children in the school year. This can mean a natural separation from those they were previously friends with, but by no means always. Two of my now teenagers are still close to some of their primary-school friends, but their circles have widened dramatically, with most of their closest friends being those they met in the last couple of years of secondary school. My other two children have moved on from their earlier friendships – no dramatic fallings-out, just a quiet transition away and forming of new relationships in their place.

Research confirms that friendships are most unstable during the period of transition between schools, finding that 73 per cent of children report a different best friend just one year after starting secondary school.[4] Keeping a close friend during the time between schools can, however, make the transition much easier for tweens, while also improving academic achievement.

Peer pressure

No chapter on friendships would be complete without a section on the peer pressure that rears its ugly head during the tween years. Peer pressure, in short, is influence from a group of peers, usually of a similar age, who may be friends or just acquaintances. When considering peer pressure, most parents think of teenagers being cajoled into trying a cigarette, alcohol or recreational drugs, but there are many other types of peer pressure that occur long before this.

Pressure to conform is all around our tweens – to support a certain football team or follow a specific pop star, to wear their hair in a particular style or sport a well-known brand of trainers ... even pencil cases and school bags don't escape peer pressure, with certain styles and brands coming into and out of fashion. Research shows that tweens are more likely than younger children or older teens to favour some styles of clothes and brands over others in order to fit in with their peers.[5] Peer-pressure-proofing your tween as much as possible now can go a long way to help in the future, should they ever find themselves as a teen in the position described above.

Peer pressure can cause tweens to do things that are otherwise very out of character. Their developing brains, low levels of impulse control and the fact that they are innately drawn to risk-taking behaviour creates a perfect storm. Often, they are seeking to fit in more, maybe because of low confidence or problematic friendships. But our tweens need to find a balance between being happy to be uniquely themselves and fitting in with others. Individuality is great and important for tweens in discovering who they are and the place they want to fill in the world, but doing things to fit in with their peers can help them to feel more confident, and this, in turn, aids their personal growth.

How do you help your tween to avoid the pitfalls of peer pressure?

- Make sure they understand what peer pressure is and why their brains are more likely to make them susceptible to it. Help them to see the negatives, and how it can inhibit their growth as a totally unique individual, and the fact that it carries risks and dangers as they approach their teen years.

- Explain to your tween that currently their brain often causes them to act first and think later. Encourage them to take a pause and consider if they are doing something because they really want to, or because they are somehow feeling pressured to comply.

- Speak with them about the fact that true friends won't ever require or urge them to change. A real friend will accept them for who they are, and allow them to say 'No' without trying to cajole them into saying 'Yes'.

- Discuss the fact that peer pressure isn't just from their friends but also from others who can influence them – for instance television, film or music stars, people they may come across on social media and adverts they are exposed to. With this in mind, it is important that they have a basic grasp of advertising and understand that very often these influencers are paid to promote something, making children feel as if they need it. It's rare that these stars use the products they are promoting.

- Talk about the fact that peer pressure isn't always negative; sometimes it can have a positive impact – by giving encouragement to take up a new hobby or try a new experience that might otherwise scare them, or by providing motivation not to quit a task that they are finding hard. Help them to recognise the difference between positive and negative peer pressure.

- Keep any discussions positive, so that they feel they can speak with you. Rein in the judgement, be open and honest (talking about a time you felt pressured by peers can help them to understand) and listen, even if you don't like what you're hearing.

- Focus on building their self-esteem, with the tips from earlier in this chapter (see page 85); if a tween is low on this, they are more likely to succumb to peer pressure.
- Give them ways to say 'No', and role-play how they may act in a situation that could be hard for them. So, if somebody is trying to get them to do something they are uncomfortable with, they could say, 'Thank you, but it's not something I want to do.' You could also suggest that they use you as an excuse if they find themselves in a particularly tricky situation, saying something like, 'Oh, my mum or dad won't let me.' You could also set up a secret code – perhaps something they say on the telephone or put in a text, to which you respond. If they are with friends and don't want to do what they are being asked to do, they could text you with a secret message, such as, 'What's for dinner?' and you would respond by phoning them and saying, 'I have to come and pick you up right now. We need to go out.'

When I talk to parents of stubborn toddlers whose favourite word is 'No!' I always tell them they'll be pleased that their child is comfortable saying 'No' when they are older, as it will help them a lot in the peer-pressure years! Now is your time to be thankful for that stubborn toddler, but the way you respond to your child now, discipline-wise, also has an impact. If your child is confident questioning your instructions, they are more likely to do the same with their peers. Remember, being able to say 'No' to their friends also means they will need to be able to say it to you, so don't rush to chastise them when they uphold an opinion that's different to yours.

It's also important to set realistic expectations of your tween when it comes to peer pressure, and not to expect more from them than you do from yourself – bear in mind that we, as adults, are not immune to it either. When was the last time you bought some make-up, a cleaning product, a health supplement or a new gadget because you saw some good reviews by somebody you follow on social media or had a conversation with a friend or colleague who recommended them? If you can identify with this, then you are most definitely still influenced by peer pressure. Why should your tween be any different?

Bullying

Bullying sadly is rife in the tween years, usually peaking between the ages of ten and thirteen. Research from the international anti-bullying charity Ditch the Label found that almost a quarter of tweens and teens surveyed said they had been bullied in the last year, with a similar number saying that they had witnessed bullying in the last year.[6] Of those who were bullied, a third said that it took place either daily, several times per week or at least weekly.

Bullying can take many forms in the tween years, and could include any of the following, from either an individual or a group of tweens:

- Physical violence
- Teasing or verbal abuse
- Deliberately excluding a tween from a friendship group
- Spreading rumours or gossiping about a tween (or group of tweens) to others
- Playing nasty jokes
- Mimicking a tween and specific characteristics they may have (for instance, their ethnicity or a disability) to others

Tweens today also have the added issue of cyberbullying to contend with. Research has found that 72 per cent of tweens and teens have felt bullied in some way online in the last year.[7] Sadly, 90 per cent of them also reported that they didn't tell their parents (or any other adult) about the bullying.

Sometimes it is obvious if a tween is being bullied – they may confess what is happening to you, or you may hear about it from their friends, siblings, other parents or school staff. Other times it is less obvious. The following are all signs that a tween may be on the receiving end of bullying:

- They become withdrawn.
- They are angrier and more short-tempered than usual.
- They are more tearful than usual or display more mood swings.
- They spend more time alone in their room, retreating from the rest of the family.
- They don't want to get involved with social events or groups they used to enjoy.
- They may try to avoid going to school.
- They may struggle to sleep.
- You may notice changes in their eating habits.
- You may notice a change in their mood after they have been using a computer, tablet or smartphone.
- They may have unexplained injuries, or their property or clothing may be damaged.

Of course, none of the above guarantees that your tween is being bullied, but any of them certainly should ring alarm bells and at least alert you to the possibility.

If your child is being bullied, or you suspect they may be, the following can help:

- Stay patient with them and their behaviour and try to keep the pressure off at home.

- Make sure they know what bullying looks like and can recognise that they are being bullied, and that it isn't right.
- Help them to realise that they should always tell you what has happened, no matter what the other child (or children) may have said to them.
- Try to stay calm and don't take matters into your own hands. You may want to go straight to the other child's (or children's) parents directly, but this can often cause far more problems for both yourself and your child, especially considering children who bully others are more likely to be bullied themselves – sometimes, sadly, their behaviour originates from their own parents, and it may escalate if you try to speak with them directly.
- Never encourage your child to hit or kick another child back or to retaliate in any other way. You may be tempted to tell them to stand up for themselves physically, but this doesn't usually solve anything and runs the risk of getting your child into trouble with the school or the group they are in.
- Teach your tween to verbally stand up for themselves and say 'Stop!' and to get adult help as soon as possible.
- Brainstorm ways in which they can respond to the bully, even role-playing them at home.
- Don't tell your daughter that if a boy is teasing her it must mean he likes her. This outdated and sexist viewpoint is sadly common, harmful and completely false.
- Encourage your tween to seek help from a trusted adult as soon as they are able to.
- Tell your tween that you would like to get as involved as they would want you to initially – don't go storming in, but make it clear if things do not get better, or they escalate, you will need to speak with their teachers or group leaders.

What to do if the bullying happens at school

You must contact the school at the earliest opportunity. Schools legally must have policies on how they deal with bullying, so if you cannot find this on their website, call and request that they provide you with a copy. Make sure you keep a written note of any bullying episodes and take notes during any meetings. This paper trail and recording is important. Most schools deal swiftly and effectively with bullying, but if you don't feel it has been addressed appropriately, your next step is to escalate the matter to the headteacher and then the board of governors. Again, putting this in writing is important, even if you meet with them in person. You will find a good resource for template letters about bullying on page 244.

What if it's your child doing the bullying?

Finding out that your own child has been bullying another is understandably heartbreaking, but please don't punish yourself too much. Often, children bully because of situations they find themselves in and peer pressure. While you may be tempted to respond to the revelation that your tween is a bully with strict authoritarian parenting, it's much better to react with understanding. As ever, your role is to find the 'why'. When you know *why* they are bullying, you are far better equipped to stop it by helping them to resolve the underlying issues. Try the following if you know (or suspect) your tween is bullying another:

- Speak up if you hear them gossiping or saying mean things about their peers; let them know that it is not kind or acceptable to say things like that about others.

- Help them to empathise with the other child and imagine how they would feel if they were on the receiving end of their own treatment.
- Investigate if they themselves are being bullied or are under peer pressure to join in with bullying. This is often the case. If they are, then the peer-pressure tips earlier in this chapter can help (see page 97).
- Remind them that even if a chat online is private it can still be screenshot and shared. Teach them: if you wouldn't say it to somebody's face, don't say it online.
- Have an honest discussion with them about why they are feeling bad (bullying is often used to make people feel better by making others feel bad).
- Encourage them to write a letter of apology to the child they have been mean to.
- Speak to the school if the bullying is happening there and ask if they have any insight into what may have triggered it.
- Work on your tween's self-esteem (see the tips on pages 85–87). Tweens who feel genuinely good about themselves are much less likely to bully others.
- If your tween is not directly doing the bullying, but is involved with a group of friends who are, help them to understand the bystander effect (see page 179) and why it's important that they don't stay quiet – even if they aren't directly doing the bullying, their lack of action can help to perpetuate it.

Friendships in the tween years can be complicated and often infuriating from the position of parent or carer, but they play a vital role in emotional and social development and can help tweens with the many transitions they face during adolescence. With a little bit of your help and a lot of your support, your tween will hopefully enjoy fulfilling and lasting friendships.

As ever though, the relationships a tween has with others are based on the one they have with you. While your tween's close friendships and desire to spend more time with friends away from your home can often make it seem that they are growing apart from you, they are actually a wonderful testament to the relationship they have with you – because the root of all relationships, including those with friends, is the parent–child one. In Chapter 13, we will look in more detail at this gradual move away from you, and how it makes you feel; but, for now, let's move on to looking a little more at your tween's feelings and their mental health.

Chapter 5

Mental Health in the Tween Years

'You are braver than you believe, stronger than you
seem, and smarter than you think.'
Pooh's Most Grand Adventure

R esearch suggests that 20 per cent of tweens and teens
experience a mental-health problem of some kind in any
given year and that 50 per cent of mental-health conditions that
affect adults are established by the age of fourteen.[1] Shocking
statistics, aren't they?

Our culture places a huge emphasis on physical health,
but far less on mental health. Thankfully, this is starting to
change, as governments begin to realise that mental health is
just as important. On the one hand, this growing awareness
is helpful for our tweens and may mean that we'll start to
see a downward shift in these statistics soon. However, the
stresses of modern life mean that there are more sources of
anxiety than perhaps ever before: climate-change anxiety,
growing up in the age of Covid-19, more standardised testing at
school, constant changes to the curriculum and the pressures

of living in an increasingly online world all take their toll on our tweens.

The good news is that being raised in a supportive and loving home where there is an awareness and acceptance of all emotions has a protective effect on tween mental health. This chapter provides a whistle-stop tour of mental-health basics in the tween years. We will look at encouraging good communication about emotions, calming anxiety, supporting tween self-care, knowing what to be on the alert for (and how) and where to go for help should you need it.

Encouraging tween emotional literacy

Emotional literacy is a phrase used to describe a person's ability to be aware of and to communicate their own feelings and understand those of others. Somebody with good emotional literacy will ultimately be able to recognise and regulate their own emotions and help others to do the same. The goal of authoritative parenting – in this context, supporting and guiding tweens – very much fits with the idea of fostering emotional literacy. Our role, as parents and carers, is threefold here:

1. We must foster good emotional literacy ourselves, because in order to contain our tweens' emotions, we must be able to contain our own, and in order to teach emotional literacy to our tweens, we must be a good role model ourselves.
2. We need to devote time to teaching our tweens about mental health, helping them to understand how their minds work and how the world around them impacts them, and guiding them towards good practices and coping strategies.

3. We need to listen to and empathise with our tweens, whatever emotion they are expressing, so that they feel safe to ask for our support when they need it.

In this chapter, we will be focusing on the teaching of emotional literacy and how to listen and support, while in Chapter 13, we will look at *your* feelings in more detail (and please don't think because this chapter comes last it is less important – it isn't).

A good place to start when explaining emotional literacy to your tween is with a discussion about brain development in adolescence. I wish that this was covered in science lessons at school but, sadly, it isn't. Although all children will learn about the basics of the brain at some point in their education, they don't learn about the direct impact of its development on them. The information we covered in Chapter 1 (see pages 10–19) should be helpful here. I have found conversations about this to be so helpful with my own children, allowing them to understand why they sometimes find it hard to regulate their feelings and behaviour – otherwise, it can be all too easy for children to blame themselves for their behaviour and for their inability to control it. The best way to communicate this information varies for all tweens: some opt to watch a short documentary aimed at their age group, some choose to read a book written for tweens, while some prefer a conversation with a parent or carer. I don't think there is any right or wrong way here – just be guided by your tween.

Another good topic to discuss with your tween is emodiversity – the concept that no feelings are bad, and all should be embraced. The idea is that we don't have to feel happy and positive all the time and we shouldn't try to chase away more difficult feelings when they appear, because experiencing a diversity of emotions – both positive and negative – is considered the most emotionally healthy. Just like biodiversity (say, a rainforest full of beautiful flora and fauna and less attractive bugs and mould), the healthiest environment emotionally is one that is a good mix of everything. Research suggests embracing emo-diversity results in less depression (and fewer treatment needs where depression is diagnosed).[2]

Along with emodiversity, I think it is a good idea to reframe the idea that happiness is the ultimate goal in life. Our tweens are bombarded with messages and adverts telling them that they should always aim to be happy, and when they don't reach this pinnacle, they wonder if there is something wrong with them. The pursuit of happiness ignores the fact that feelings of content-ment, calm, amusement and just feeling OK are all positive, too. Indeed, research shows that adults who experience a full range of positive emotions, not just happy, are potentially healthier with less susceptibility to disease.[3]

Perhaps the golden rule to teach your tween is that we should be encouraged to embrace and express all of our feel-ings. No emotions are bad; it's how you express and regulate them that matters. For instance, anger is not a negative emo-tion, but screaming at somebody when they make you angry is unacceptable. This is something we'll look at a little more later in the chapter.

Encouraging your tween to talk about their emotions

It's common for tweens to spend hours alone in their bed-rooms in the evenings and at weekends, and for questions to be answered with grunts of just 'Yes' or 'No'. It's unsurprising, then, that many parents are unsure how to encourage their tweens to open up about their emotions, when they can't even get them to tell them what they did at school on any given day. Here are a few tips to make things a little easier:

- Pick a time when your tween is calm and relaxed naturally – just before bedtime is good, or over lunch or dinner if you eat together. Don't carve out a specific time and say, 'I'd like to have a talk', as this can make them feel pressured and far less likely to want to discuss things with you.
- Practise active listening, by which I mean knowing when to be quiet (which is usually most of the time), when to ask questions and what questions to ask. Open-ended questions, such as, 'Can you tell me how you are feeling at the moment?' are much better than those which only require a 'Yes' or 'No' answer.
- Show empathy, but don't pretend that you know exactly how they are feeling. You might say something like, 'That sounds really tough; it seems that you are very anxious when you are at school', rather than, 'Oh, I used to feel like that at your age, too.'
- Don't be dismissive, even if you think you are doing it to help. You may be tempted to say something like, 'Don't worry, everything will be OK', but this diminishes their feelings without actually helping them.
- Hold back on giving advice immediately and instead ask how they would like you to help.
- Talk openly and honestly about your own emotions on a regular basis. Showing by example that talking about feelings is welcome and natural in your family is perhaps the best way to encourage them to talk to you.
- If they can't open up to you verbally, use alternative ways that make them more comfortable – perhaps email, text messages or even writing notes to each other in a book passed between the two of you.
- Fill your home with positive and inspiring quotes and messages and choose books and watch TV shows or films about mental health together. Disney Pixar's *Inside Out* is

a must-watch for parents of tweens and tweens alike as it looks at emotions in a very approachable and helpful way. It's fun, too!

- Don't expect them to tell you everything all at once. Be patient. It's much better that they tell you a little at a time, than you pressure them to disclose the big picture all in one go and risk them clamming up.

Ultimately, your best approach to raising an emotionally literate tween, who values and accepts emodiversity, is to be accepting of your own emotions as well as theirs and to raise them in an environment where everybody's feelings are accepted and nurtured. This can be particularly hard if you were brought up in a home where exclusion methods of discipline were used (such as being sent to your room if you were angry or rude to your parents), but consider yourself a work in progress: you don't have to get everything right straight away. If your tween says or does something in an emotive episode that triggers you and you are tempted to discipline them using a method based on exclusion or punishment, you should take time away from them to calm down, reflect on your actions, take a breath and remind yourself that it's time for you to be the adult. You know what you need to do: apologise; tell them you are sorry you overreacted and that you love and support them whatever emotions they have and ask if you can have a chat about what happened with them. Remember, as an adult, your goal is to help them to regulate their emotions, not make things worse with your own emotional dysregulation. Take as much time as you need to calm down and regroup before apologising and starting afresh.

TOXIC MASCULINITY AND WHY
WE'RE HURTING YOUNG BOYS

In the UK, 75 per cent of all suicides are men,[4] and a third of men are too embarrassed to seek or accept help for mental-health issues.[5] Male mental health is a ticking time bomb. By adulthood, men have been subject to a huge amount of negative societal conditioning, telling them how they should behave and how they should (or shouldn't) feel. To improve things, we need to start at the beginning of life, with boys.

We encourage a far narrower range of emotions in men than we do in women. The term 'toxic masculinity' describes the common stereotypes society applies to men, boys and masculinity and the accepted social norms that are harmful to them. It does not imply that masculinity itself is bad, but rather the beliefs and actions that can accompany it. For instance, the expectation that it is less masculine to cry and show emotions, or the use of the phrase 'man up'.

Toxic masculinity is rife in our society and these norms, so often unconsciously repeated, have an incredibly negative impact on tween boys. How do we avoid it with them? We need them to understand that it's OK to have feelings, it's OK to share them and it's OK to ask for help, regardless of your sex. We need to stop using outdated masculine language with our tweens, such as 'be a man', 'grow some balls', 'don't be a sissy', 'be a brave soldier' and so on, because it really affects them, perpetuating the stereotypical belief that it is somehow emasculating to show emotions. We also need to stop blaming so-called 'boisterous' and difficult behaviour on testosterone (this is a myth, as we saw on page 24) and expect better of and for boys. We need to embrace our tween boys as they are and allow them to be who they want to be, not try to shape them into 'little men'.

Even if we think we aren't stereotyping our boys, we most likely are. We ourselves are conditioned by those who came before us. We subconsciously select the building or fighting toys, the cars, the planes, the trains and the dinosaurs. We subconsciously buy them books about pirates, knights, warriors and superheroes. We buy them clothing in dark blue, black, grey and army green, emblazoned with logos and slogans about being brave or strong. And we speak to them very differently from the way in which we talk to girls. Research shows that parents of boys naturally engage in less conversation with them and speak less about emotions with them when they do, compared to parents of girls.[6] If we want to save our boys from toxic masculinity, communication and conversation about emotions is perhaps the best way forward. Once again, our goal as parents is to teach emotional literacy and encourage full emodiversity, whatever the child's sex.

THE PROBLEM WITH GIRLS BEING SUGAR AND SPICE AND ALL THINGS NICE

Just as we run the risk of creating emotional problems for our boys by gender stereotyping and steering them away from what society believes is 'feminine behaviour', we also harm our girls with similar stereotypes.

As a child, I was often referred to as 'bossy'. I realise now that what was really meant by this was that I stood up for myself, I called out behaviour and treatment I didn't like and I was often assertive when with other children. Had I been a boy, I probably would have been called 'strong' or 'brave' and been congratulated on my leadership skills. As a girl, however, these characteristics were not considered feminine.

Girls are subconsciously taught from a young age to be sweet and submissive. If they enjoy so-called 'masculine' pastimes or activities or they prefer to wear jeans and trainers to skirts and dresses, they are considered tomboys – an indication, again, that they are somehow not feminine enough.

What impact does this have on our girls? It can create an inner turmoil, where they struggle to suppress their true personalities in a quest to fit into the world around them. This can cause unhappiness and anxiety, after years of living inauthentically. Our daughters may be afraid to speak up for themselves for fear of being perceived as 'unfeminine', and those who do not fit with the hyper-feminine gender stereotype may question if there is something wrong with them, rather than understanding that any problems rest solely with society. Steering girls towards always acting and – importantly – looking 'nice' (for 'nice' read 'pretty') with an unhealthy focus on their appearance can also cause huge issues with body image as they grow, something we will look at in much more depth later (see pages 152–154).

The world would really be a much better place, and our girls so much happier, if we could resist labelling them and trying to direct their behaviour to be more 'girly'.

Fostering resilience in tweens

Resilience is a word often used to describe the ability to stay focused and calm and to keep trying, even if you fail. It basically means picking yourself up and dusting yourself off again and again, until you succeed. Resilience is intricately linked to self-esteem: if you feel good about yourself, you're more likely to stick at something that you're finding tricky. And the same is true for our tweens.

Therefore, to foster resilience, we first need to work on self-esteem and self-confidence. We looked at self-esteem in Chapter 4 so do flip back to refresh yourself if needed (see pages 85–87.) For now, I'd like to focus on the idea of mindsets and how what we think about ourselves can – and does – impact the outcome of a challenge.

Professor Carol Dweck, a psychologist based at Stanford University in the USA, introduced the world to her theory of mindset in her book of the same name.[7] The theory states that success and achievement are based not on innate ability but upon the individual's *beliefs* surrounding their ability to achieve. Dweck identified two main mindsets: fixed and growth.

An individual with a fixed mindset believes that abilities and capabilities are innate and that nothing can really be done to change them. They feel that failure is an indication that they are not good enough, and that, as such, it is something to be feared and avoided, if possible. This fear of failure means that they tend to give up easily when they feel a task is too hard for them. A fixed mindset is summed up by this sort of thinking: *I can't do this. I'm not good enough. I should just give up.*

An individual with a growth mindset believes that abilities are not fixed and that they can always be improved with hard work and determination. They view failure as an indication that they did not try hard enough, and therefore they don't take it badly or fear it – instead, they welcome it as a learning opportunity. And because they don't fear failure or believe it is inevitable, they will be more determined and focused on a task that they find challenging, sticking with it until they have mastered it. A growth mindset is summed up by this way of thinking: *I can't do this yet. I believe I can if I try, though.*

Dweck's mindset theory applies at any age, but often starts to manifest more in the tween years than in the earlier years, when children tend to be innately optimistic and veer towards a growth mindset naturally. Mindsets are by no means permanent; it is possible to change from one to another, and we all commonly alternate between the two over time. It's unlikely that your tween will be conscious of the mindset they hold most often, although educating them about the idea can help them to become more aware. As a parent or carer, you can easily notice when your tween is stuck in a fixed mindset, and if this happens, pointing it out can be helpful. You can also encourage a growth mindset with the following tips:

- Help your tween to accept that we all fail at times – it's just part of life – but it doesn't mean that we will always fail.
- Empathise with their feelings when things don't go well and show that you understand that they feel bad. Don't dismiss their emotions by saying something like, 'Oh well, better luck next time.' Of course, focusing on the ability to do better in the future is important in fostering a growth mindset, but not at the expense of empathising and listening to how a child is feeling first.
- Help them to see the positives in failure: we would never learn how to master things if we didn't learn to see what we needed to change because of failure.
- Don't praise or reward them based on outcome (for instance, don't praise or reward a grade A for a piece of schoolwork over a C that they worked hard for); instead, focus on the effort that they put into doing something, regardless of the outcome.
- Help them to recognise what they did to succeed at doing something. For example, what did they do differently? Again, this takes the focus back to the process and the hard work put in, not the outcome itself.

- Share your own failures with them, it's important that they see you aren't always successful and that when you do mess up you own it and move on. However, be aware that the aim here is to help them to see you are human, not to dismiss their experience or presume that yours is the same.

- Look at stories of overcoming adversity together – can you find inspiring ones about people who initially didn't succeed, or followed a tough path in life, yet rose above these difficulties to succeed and be happy? When you do come across a story like this, focus on all the hard work put in and how people don't automatically always succeed at something and how it's OK if it takes time to do so (this often makes the story much more inspiring).

Helping to foster a growth mindset in your tween will have a positive impact on their self-esteem and self-confidence, and recognising the different mindsets when they occur goes a long way to nurturing their developing emotional literacy.

Coping with big feelings

As adults, when we feel tricky emotions, we are usually adept at working out what we are feeling and why, and our developed brains allow us to rationally think about the best response. However, at some point, we have all acted out in the grip of big, raw emotions in ways that we are probably not proud of – because we are all human. Therefore, we should not expect more of our tweens; in fact, we should expect a lot less, because they don't have fully developed adult brains. We'll look at some tips soon for tweens coping 'in the moment', but first, I think it's import-ant to consider how we can help our tweens to understand and recognise their emotions, especially anxiety (often confused with other emotions, such as anger).

I always talk to tweens about recognising the physical sensations of anxiety and knowing what they may indicate. It's also a good idea to explain what is happening in their bodies at the time to cause the physical reactions. Talk about the following:

- Butterflies in the tummy
- Sweating and clammy palms
- Quick, shallow breathing and shortness of breath
- A dry mouth, with a lump in the throat
- Tummy ache and sometimes diarrhoea
- Nausea
- Shaking and trembling
- Increased heart rate and a pounding sensation in the chest
- Paleness or flushing of the skin

These physical manifestations of anxiety can be really scary for tweens, which, in turn, can make the anxiety worse. I would recommend briefly explaining the fight-or-flight response to them, saying that when we are scared of something (real or imagined) or stressed, our bodies release catecholamines (the hormones adrenaline and noradrenaline), which prepare the body to either run quickly or stay and fight the perceived (or real) threat. In order to run away quickly or stay and fight, we need blood and oxygen in the most important parts of the body (heart, lungs and brain), so it is diverted or drawn away from areas that are less important (which is why we look pale when we are scared). We also need to be on high alert, with all our focus on running quickly or fighting hard, so those body systems that are less important for our immediate survival (like the gastrointestinal system) shut down temporarily, causing us to have a tummy ache and need to go to the toilet lots or to feel (or be) sick. Demystifying these bodily responses to fear,

anxiety or stress can help tweens to recognise what they are feeling and why, while being mindful of these sensations can help them to know when to use techniques to calm themselves. This element of control can be so empowering for them, and although it may not remove the big feelings, it can help with managing them.

CLIMATE-CHANGE ANXIETY

I remember distinctly when I learned about climate change at secondary school: I remember the exact desk I was sitting at, I remember the teacher's voice and I remember feeling horrified at the impending doom our world was facing. It hit me hard. Things have changed a lot since that moment over thirty years ago. They have got worse. A lot, lot worse. Our tweens today have good reason to be anxious about the climate and their future. A survey of 2000 eight- to sixteen-year olds, commissioned by the BBC, found that most children are worried about the impact climate change will have on them and one in five has nightmares about it.[8] It's important not to dismiss your child's climate-change worries, not least because you could inadvertently make them worse, but also because climate change is a very real fact, and tweens are clever enough, and have enough independent exposure to the world, to know if you are lying, which could diminish their trust in you. The best way forward is to acknowledge their fears and ask how they might use them to fire up a positive growth mindset. When tweens feel involved and feel like they are doing something to make the world better it is a huge help to their anxiety. You could suggest that they get involved with positive-change or awareness projects (something we will examine in Chapter 9, when we look at tween activism) or speak with their school about starting a climate-change-awareness project. You could also have a family meeting about ways you could change your ecological impact in your own home.

COVID ANXIETY

The world changed unimaginably in 2020 with the Covid-19 pandemic. For our tweens, unexpected time off school may have initially been welcomed, but the lack of a regular routine, the absence of their friends and the unpredictability of emergency lockdown schooling at home (note: I haven't called this home-schooling or home-education as these both involve a great deal of planning and socialising, neither of which was involved in lockdown schooling) understandably hit them hard. Our tweens have gone through something none of us ever did at their age and I don't think we can dismiss the impact of the pandemic, even if your family remained healthy and as happy as possible throughout it. Here, the answer is time and showing patience with them, while they process what happened. Anxiety can have an impact on behaviour, underpinning it for many months – even years – afterwards, but, irrespective of the source, anxiety it is, and the approach to dealing with it is the same as addressing any other type of anxiety, namely, with under-standing, support and finding ways to empower tweens to manage it.

Some quick and easy coping strategies

The following techniques can be helpful in times when your tween is feeling consumed by big emotions, whatever the emotion may be, although they are especially useful for reducing anxiety and feelings of anger. Take some time to practise them with your tween when they are calm, so they will have the tools to use independently when they need them.

I-spy senses

Mindfulness, or being aware of your surroundings and focusing on the present, can really help you to feel calm. I-spy senses involves your tween focusing on what they can hear, see, touch and smell at any one time. Explain that they should ask themselves, 'What's one thing I can *hear* right now?' Then, 'What's one thing I can *see* right now?' and 'What's one thing I can *feel* right now?' And finally, 'What's one thing I can *smell* right now?' They can challenge themselves and see how many of each they can identify.

The worry meter

Ask your tween to imagine that they have a dial in their head – a bit like the one in a car that shows when you need to get petrol. But instead of saying 'empty' (on the left), it says 'calm'; and instead of saying full (on the right), it says 'worry'. Ask them where their needle is pointing to right now? If they aren't feeling calm, ask if they can imagine turning the dial down a little bit with their mind and their breathing. Suggest that they imagine the pointer moving towards 'calm'. They can focus on breathing out to move the dial, seeing it go down a little with every big, slow breath out.

Balloon breathing

Ask your tween to imagine that they are going to blow up a huge balloon. Tell them to close their eyes and picture the balloon in front of them in their favourite colour. Next, they should take a big breath in (they will need to have enough air to fill that balloon!), hold it a second while they picture bringing the balloon to their mouth, then imagine they are blowing into that balloon and it's getting bigger and bigger. When they run out of air, they should take another breath in, and then carry on blowing up the balloon until it is full. If they are still anxious after filling up the first balloon, they can imagine blowing up more than one, then either letting them go and watching them float off into the sky or collecting lots of brightly coloured balloons on the floor around them.

4:8 breathing

Sometimes it can be hard to picture things in your imagination. If this is the case for your tween, they can simply count as they breathe in and out slowly. This works best if they breathe in and out through their nose, breathing in to the count of 4 (1-2-3-4) and then out to the count of 8 (1-2-3-4-5-6-7-8). Repeat as many times as needed, until they start to feel calmer. Closing their eyes when they do this can make it even more effective.

Superhero helpers

This is a lovely idea for younger tweens, specifically those aged ten and under. Explain to them that when we are scared or worried about something, our bodies release something called hormones, which can make us feel a bit funny. They can give us butterflies in our tummies, make our throats feel dry and even make our hearts beat quicker. These feelings can sometimes make us feel more scared, but they are the body's way of trying to help us to cope with whatever is scaring us and of staying safe. Sometimes, though, the body gets a bit confused and releases these hormones when it doesn't need to – when what we fear isn't going to hurt us. Explain to them that it can help to imagine a worry or fear as a superhero, trying to save them – only they're a bit of a silly superhero and sometimes they respond when they don't need to. Suggest to your tween that they may want to give their inner superhero a name and the next time they appear, they can choose to say, 'Thank you, [insert chosen name], for helping me, but I am OK and don't need you right now.' They can imagine them zooming off into the distance, ready to help on another day. They could even draw a cartoon of their inner superhero and hang it in their bedroom to help them to visualise it.

Positive affirmations

Affirmations are positive statements about yourself that you read or memorise and then repeat, either out loud or in your mind. The theory is that, repeated often enough, these affirmations will convince your subconscious mind that they are true. The more you practise them, the greater the effect. Affirmations work best for your tween if they can write their own, unique to their situation, perhaps with your help. However, don't let this be a hurdle – if they are not keen on this idea, there are plenty of pre-made positive-affirmation cards you can purchase and many that you can print off the internet for free. You can also access pre-recorded audio versions of affirmations, which are great to listen to at night as your tween drifts off to sleep in bed.

Here are some ideas for positive affirmations:

- 'I am confident, I am calm.'
- 'I feel safe and loved.'

- 'I believe in myself.'
- 'I am doing the best I can, and my best is good enough.'
- 'I am proud of myself.'
- 'I am enough as I am.'

Gratitude lists

This idea follows on a little from positive affirmations, but instead of your tween thinking about themselves in a positive way, the emphasis this time is on the world around them and all that is good in it. Focusing on gratitude is a great way to feel more positive. Some choose to consider things they are grateful for as soon as they wake up in the morning, to set the day on a good footing, whereas others choose to focus on gratitude at bedtime, so they go to sleep with a feeling of peace. If a whole list seems too daunting, ask your tween to name just one thing they are grateful for each day. This is lovely as a daily practice for the two of you to take part in.

Journaling

Journaling is a little like keeping a diary, but instead of focusing on what has happened each day, it is more about how you feel each day. There are no rules to follow, no specific journals to buy, no list of what must be written and no schedule for how often to write. Journaling is a great way for your tween to offload feelings that they may not want to talk about, or it can also be used as a communication tool between the two of you, with you responding to your tween's entries, or even writing down your own next to theirs, if they want to share and not keep their thoughts private. If they do want to keep their journal private, however, you really must respect this and not be tempted to sneak a peek at any point.

Daily goal setting

Encourage your tween to write a daily goal at the start of each day; they could do this in a journal or on a piece of coloured card. They should focus on just one small thing that they want to achieve for the day. This could be as simple as 'try to stay calm today' or 'take big breaths if I feel anxious' or 'aim to smile or laugh at least once'. The goal doesn't have to be huge – in fact, smaller goals are much more achievable and therefore, overall, more positive when they are regularly achieved. When your tween accomplishes their goal (and this doesn't have to be on the day it was set), they could put the piece of card into a special jar or treasure chest, or hang it in their room with mini pegs on a piece of string. Collecting all their achieved goals can really help to bolster their confidence on days when they are feeling down, as they serve as a reminder of what they are capable of.

Random acts of kindness

Helping others and showing kindness towards them helps us to release feel-good hormones. Your tween could take some cupcakes they have baked to school, to share with their classmates, make a card to send to a friend or relative or paint a rock with a special message to leave on a local bench for others to find.

Art

Some tweens aren't huge fans of writing but can get a great sense of release from arts-and-crafts projects. Painting and drawing feelings can be incredibly therapeutic. The calming effects of the quiet concentration can help with anxiety and the freedom of being able to use different media in whatever style works best for them can help to release anger in safety.

Listening to or making music

Music can have a profound effect on the body, reducing blood pressure and heart rate and encouraging alpha waves – the state of relaxation – in the brain. It isn't just stereotypically calming music that helps though; listening to loud rock or dance music can help to release difficult emotions, too, especially if there are lyrics that tweens can relate to. Playing an instrument or singing is also a wonderful way to calm emotions.

Gardening

Spending time in nature is so important for all of us. Giving your tween a plant or some seeds to nurture can focus their attention and help them to relax. If you have a garden, you could section off a small area for your tween to cultivate in whatever way they like. But you don't have to have a garden or outdoor space; you can buy small herb planter pots and seeds to grow on your kitchen windowsill – you just need light and water. It would be great if they could choose some herbs that they like, and when it's time to harvest them, to use them in cooking their favourite meal.

Self-care for tweens

Self-care has become a real buzz word recently, particularly when it comes to parenting. Pick up any magazine that focuses on well-being or parenting (or read any similarly themed website) and within a few articles you will find one professing the benefits of self-care and why you should do it. What you don't see, however, are articles on self-care for tweens or even teens, yet it is just as important for them as it is for us as adults.

The four key pillars of self-care at any age are eating well, sleeping well, moving well and thinking well of yourself. We will look at eating, sleeping and moving (exercise) in the tween years in Chapters 7 and 8. Thinking well of yourself simply means cutting yourself a break: understanding and accepting that everybody has faults, everybody has down days and everybody messes up sometimes – and that these things don't mean you are flawed; they mean you are human.

Some tweens can have issues with perfectionism and this psychological type of self-care is crucial for them. This encompasses the ideas of growth mindsets and mindfulness – recognising that it's OK to make mistakes, learn from them and try again, and being mindful of your feelings in the current moment.

On the topic of self-care, I strongly endorse the idea of having a mental-health day now and again. If we wake in the morning and we have an upset stomach or a fever, we will call in sick to work and retreat to our beds or relax on the sofa. We need to treat our mental health in the same way and recognise that sometimes we need to take the day to focus on it. I have allowed all my children to take mental-health days and stay home from school if needed. I would aim for them to have only one per term, but if they needed more, that was OK. Some may worry that their tweens will push the boundaries and try to stay home more often, but it just doesn't work like that. My children and I trusted each other and they only ever asked if they really felt the need to stay at home. On my part, I believed them whenever they asked – after all, they were the ones inside their own heads, not me. So if they asked for a day at home, they obviously needed it and I had no qualms about calling the school and telling them that they were having a day off sick for mental-health reasons. And I was never challenged on it.

When and how to seek professional help

Sometimes mental-health issues in tweens become too big for families to handle alone. If you sense that you or your tween are struggling to the extent that you don't feel confident moving forwards alone and you are not seeing any positive change, then please don't hesitate to seek professional help. I think trusting your instinct is the most important guide, but if you are unsure, erring on the side of caution is usually better. I would seek professional help if my child were showing any of the following:

- **Signs of depression** – including withdrawal, no longer doing things they previously enjoyed, changes in appetite, sleep or behaviour, especially irritability and anger or sadness and changes in achievement at school.
- **Signs of self-harm** – including unexplained scratches, bites, cuts, burns and bruises, hitting or punching walls or themselves. They may wear long-sleeved clothing more, even during a hot summer, to cover up any marks, or you may find blood stains or bloodied tissues in their room or the bathroom.
- **Signs of post-traumatic stress disorder (PTSD)** – including an increase in nightmares, flashbacks to, or intrusive memories of, a traumatic event and signs of hypervigilance or hyperarousal, where they are often on high alert and jumpy, and attempts to avoid situations that are similar to that in which the traumatic event occurred.
- **Signs of generalised anxiety disorder (GAD)** – including intense, almost constant worry that may not have an identifiable cause, or is more intense than the situation usually calls for, sleeping problems, changes to

eating habits, lots of stomach aches and headaches, extreme separation anxiety when away from you, and school refusal.

- **Suicidal thoughts** – including comments about potentially ending things being a way out, exclaiming that there is no point in living or saying that others would be better off if they were dead; expressing ideas of suicide in writing or in drawings or doodles; or more risk-taking, dangerous behaviour, social withdrawal and attempts to say goodbye to friends or family.
- **Eating disorders** – including avoidance of family mealtimes or disappearing as soon as they are over, an obsession with weight or body size, calories or nutrient content of food, a fixation with an increasing amount of exercise, strict dieting, overeating as a coping mechanism for stress and food wrappers hidden in their room or school bag.

If you feel that the tips provided earlier in this book are not helping, or that things are escalating, you should seek professional advice and help. Early professional intervention is crucial with tween mental-health issues. The sooner you can get appropriate help, the more positive the outcome. If it is an emergency, don't hesitate to call the emergency services or attend accident and emergency at your local hospital. Otherwise, your first point of call is usually your family doctor, who will listen and make a referral to the appropriate adolescent mental-health services. Some of these services also allow parents to self-refer, without needing to go through a GP – in England, for example, you can search online for your local Emotional Wellbeing and Mental Health Service (EWMHS). Schools can also refer you for many mental-health and wellbeing services if you would prefer to speak with them first. There are also many support organisations who run free telephone helplines, online chat services and local support groups. You can find a list of some of these (in the UK) in the Resources on page 243.

In February 2015, the Duchess of Cambridge was quoted as saying:

> A child's mental health is just as important as their physical health and deserves the same quality of support. No one would feel embarrassed about seeking help for a child if they broke their arm and we really should be equally ready to support a child coping with emotional difficulties.[9]

I think all parents would do well to take this to heart. As a society, we must be more aware and supportive of mental health – not only that of our children, but our own, too (something we will look at in Chapter 13). We must value and nurture our tween's mental health as much as we do their physical health. For most, this will mean being mindful of our own words and actions on a daily basis, conscious of our tween's feelings and how they are handling them and providing extra support when we think it is necessary. Sometimes this extra support will need to come from professionals, and we should never hesitate to contact them.

Next, in Chapter 6, we look at love, sexual identity, body autonomy and romantic relationships.

Chapter 6

Love, Identity and Body Autonomy

'Love is love is love is love is love is love is love is love.'

LIN-MANUEL MIRANDA,
composer, lyricist and actor

Do you remember the first time you fell in love? I remember being seven years old and kissing a big poster of George Michael on my bedroom wall every night. I was convinced we would meet, fall in love and marry one day. My imaginary love affair with George gave way a couple of years later to a crush on a real-life boy in my class at school. I watched him every lunchtime from across the playground, with big puppy-dog eyes, and imagined what it would be like to hold his hand. My heart was crushed after a few weeks, however, when he started to date another girl in my class. I vividly remember how jealous and let down I felt. How could he fall in love with her? Didn't he know we were meant to be together? The rest of my tween years remained full of unrequited crushes until I met my first boyfriend at thirteen. I felt so grown-up when we went on our first date (accompanied by one of my friends and two of his) and he bought me a pair of 99p fake Ray-Ban sunglasses, before we went to his house and watched a film, snuggling close together on the sofa with our friends either side of us. Once again, I was convinced we were made for each other, until I decided – two weeks later – that I had gone off him. Only, I was too embarrassed to end things with him, so my best friend did it for me.

First love and all that it brings with it can be wonderful, but also bittersweet. The tween heart can be fickle, fragile and easily hurt. To a tween, relationships and infatuations feel so very real, even though as adults we know that they are fleeting at that age. Yet, this realness, and often rawness, can – and does – shape us. I wouldn't be the same without my first experiences of love in my tween years; you wouldn't be either. And it's not just the objects of our affections that change us. The way our parents connect and communicate with us about them sets the foundations for our future relationships, with ourselves and others, too.

In this chapter, we will look at how to help your tween through these first experiences, including coping with unrequited crushes and being dumped, as well as promoting body autonomy, supporting tweens who identify as LGBTQ+ and speaking to tweens about sex, relationships and consent.

Self-love and positive relationships

If you could give your tween one piece of advice about future romantic relationships, what would it be? Mine would be: you must always start with loving yourself. Self-love, I believe, must be the first step in any positive relationship. If you love and respect yourself, then you will demand that same love and respect from others. In previous chapters, we looked at helping tweens with their self-esteem, which is such an important part of setting off on any future romantic relationships, too. Of course, how they treat others is also important, and my mantra has always been: 'treat others how you want to be treated'. Raising a tween with authoritative parenting is another way to set a great example for future romantic relationships – because if tweens are used to being treated with empathy and respect, the hope is that they will naturally be that way with others.

I think it's important to chat to tweens about what to look for in a positive relationship and any red flags that they should watch out for. It's never too early to make them alert to the signs of a toxic or abusive relationship. If they start with expecting the best for themselves, I genuinely believe it will help them going forwards into adulthood.

The following are signs of a positive relationship that I would make tweens aware of:

- Both people trust each other.
- Both people respect each other.
- There is good, open, honest communication between both people.
- Both people enjoy being together and have fun.
- Each partner has their own separate identity away from the other.
- Both people support each other.
- Both people treat each other fairly and equally.
- Being with your partner brings you more happiness and joy than stress and worry.

The following are signs of a toxic or abusive relationship to make tweens aware of:

- A lack of trust, or dishonest behaviour.
- Controlling behaviour, such as controlling or stopping friendships with others.
- One or both people feel insecure.

- Avoiding all conflict and disagreements.
- Co-dependency, where both are overly dependent on each other.
- The relationship often causes stress or worry.
- One person's needs are put before the other's.
- There is pressure to change who you are, or what you enjoy.
- Any signs of violence (which can include verbal violence and controlling behaviour). It's important to understand that while many presume that most violence in a relationship comes from males, it can also come from females.

Remind your tween that it's always good to check in on how they feel when they are with their partner and if anything doesn't quite feel right, to trust their instinct. Also reiterate that if ever they need to talk about a relationship with you, you're always happy to listen unjudgementally and give advice if they ask for it.

Unrequited crushes, dumping and ghosting

Heartbreak sadly comes with the territory of first loves. Whether a tween is in love with somebody who doesn't love them back, their partner breaks up with them or they are more callously ghosted (where they are completely ignored by their partner – a form of breaking up without the actual break-up conversation), parents and carers should remember that the resulting feelings are very real to them. In your adult world, with your adult worries, it can be all too easy to dismiss their heartache with a quick, 'Oh, never mind. You're so young still. It was never serious – you'll meet someone else!' And although the likelihood is that this is true, to your tween this was their one true love. It was and is a big deal. So telling them that there are plenty more fish in the sea won't help, and it could make them less likely to open up to you about future relationship issues.

The best way to respond? Listen empathetically, let them talk as much as they need to, give them a big box of tissues, a huge hug and ask if they fancy doing something special with you. If they prefer to stay in their room and cry, let them. You could also use some of the strategies outlined in the previous chapter for coping with anxiety (see pages 121–126) – they work equally well with other big feelings, like heartbreak.

If Your tween is LGBTQ+

LGBTQ+ stands for the lesbian, gay, bisexual, transgender, queer and others community. Sometimes you will see this abbreviated to just LGBT (lesbian, gay, bisexual and transgender) or LGBTQ (lesbian, gay, bisexual, transgender and queer). However, LGBTQ+ is considered a more inclusive acronym.

COMMON LGBTQ+ TERMS

The following is a list of some LGBTQ+ terms that you may not have come across before, or perhaps not fully understood:

- **Sex** – used to define somebody's biological traits, such as chromosomes and primary sex characteristics.
- **Gender** – used to define somebody's personal identity and the social and cultural constructions around what it is to be feminine or masculine. For most people, their sex and their gender align.

- **Gender identity** – how an individual perceives themselves, e.g. as a woman, a man, or something else.
- **Gender expression** – used to describe how an individual expresses themselves in terms of their gender identity.
- **Gender fluid** – used to describe an individual whose gender identity and expression shift with fluidity between two or more genders.
- **Non-binary** – used to describe somebody who does not identify with either stereotypical traditional male or female genders. Some may feel that they are somewhere between both; others may fluctuate between one and the other; and some may feel they have no gender at all (sometimes temporarily, or sometimes permanently).
- **Pansexual** – used to describe somebody whose attraction and connection with others is not limited by sex, gender or gender identity. Sometimes these individuals refer to themselves as '**gender-blind**', meaning that they do not notice gender, only the individual person.
- **Queer** – used as an umbrella term to describe the orientations, identities, sexual preferences and habits of those who don't consider themselves part of the monogamous, heterosexual majority of society. Queer can be a derogatory term when used as a slur against gay men and lesbians, and although it has now been reclaimed with pride by much of the LGBTQ+ community, its use by those outside of it can still be considered an insult.
- **Genderqueer** – used to denote a gender identity that falls into the umbrella of 'queer', i.e. those typically outside of heterosexual or homosexual norms. The term can be used to describe a person's sexual orientation or non-binary gender identity.

- **Heteronormative** – used to describe the viewpoint that heterosexuality (opposite-sex attraction) is the default and often preferred mode of sexual orientation in society.
- **Transgender** – used to describe a person who identifies as a member of the opposite sex to that which they were born.
- **Cisgender** (or cis for short) – used for those who are not transgender, i.e. their birth sex and gender are aligned.

What should parents do if they believe their tween may be LGBTQ+?

All parents should be supportive of their tweens, providing unconditional love and acceptance, something I have stressed lots in this book so far. However, this is even more important if you think your tween may identify as LGBTQ+. Of course, even if your tween doesn't identify as LGBTQ+, you should still want to raise an ally (that is, a heterosexual, or straight, cisgender individual who backs equal civil rights and gender equality and stands up and supports those in the LGBTQ+ community), and we will look at this more in Chapter 9.

The following are important to consider:

- Check your own biases. Most of us were raised in a heteronormative world, rife with homophobia and transphobia. Those in the UK who attended school between 1988 and 2003 would have been affected by Margaret Thatcher's government's Section 28. This was a clause prohibiting councils and, most importantly, schools from so-called 'promotion' of homosexuality, with Thatcher famously saying: 'Children who need to be taught to respect traditional moral values are being taught that they have an inalienable right to be gay. All of those children are being cheated of a sound start in life.' This meant that sex education and related support in schools and from social-care services legally had to avoid all LGBTQ+ issues, resulting in widespread bullying and homophobia. The law was abolished in 2000 in Scotland and in 2003 in England and Wales, but those who grew up in the Section 28 era, could be – and were – affected, and it is very possible that you have some conscious or unconscious biases because of it. As with all aspects of parenting, you must confront these beliefs and how they may affect your child and your relationship with them.

- Don't make assumptions about your tween, their sexuality or gender identity. Your assumption may be entirely incorrect, and regardless of what you believe, your tween may identify differently, or may not yet fully understand.

- Tweens can and do experiment with their gender identities and expressions of it, but never indicate to them that it is 'just a phase', no matter how positively you try to phrase it. This stage may pass, or it may not. And for those for whom it doesn't pass, the labelling of their identity as a phase is extremely damaging.

- Be open and encourage conversation. Let your tween know that you are always happy to talk with them about anything, or just listen, but never pressure them into conversations, or try to encourage them to 'out' themselves. Even if you believe that your tween is LGBTQ+, wait for them to broach it with you in their own way and in their own time.

- Make sure your tween knows that you love them uncon-ditionally, no matter who they are, or who they may be attracted to. Your love and support of them will never change. Also, don't presume that they instinctively know this. Tell them often.
- Be positive about differences and celebrate all sorts of families and couples. Let them know that you value love and identity in all its glorious differences. Actively search out television programmes, films and books fea-turing those from the LGBTQ+ community and make it a normal part of your family life to demonstrate acceptance.
- Call out friends and other family members for homo-phobia and transphobia and check yourself if you say something that could be offensive. Allowing negative talk from others can lead LGBTQ+ tweens to develop something known as internalised homophobia or trans-phobia (where they themselves believe it is wrong and hugely struggle with their feelings and identity).
- Don't talk with your tweens about when they grow up and 'get a boyfriend' or 'get a girlfriend'. This language assumes that they are heterosexual and is part of our heteronormative culture. Instead, use inclusive lan-guage – 'Whoever you may love when you are older' or, 'When you get a boyfriend or a girlfriend'.
- If and when your tween does 'come out' to you, don't stop talking about potential romantic partners. Some parents can feel uncomfortable and so stop mentioning future loves altogether, but this lack of conversation can be keenly felt by LGBTQ+ tweens.
- Don't mention any concern you may have for them as a LGBTQ+ tween. You wouldn't mention concerns if they were heterosexual, so there is no need to mention it if they are LGBTQ+. If you do have worries, remember,

they are yours, not those of your tween. Sharing with them will not help them but could hurt them.

- Following on from the above point, don't raise concerns that you won't become a grandparent or similar. Once again, there is no guarantee of grandchildren if your children are heterosexual cisgendered and there are many ways for LGBTQ+ individuals to become parents.
- Don't presume friends of the opposite sex are always romantic or tease your tween about it. Similarly, if your tween does tell you that they are attracted to those of the same sex, don't presume they are attracted to all their same-sex friends. If you are straight, you are not automatically attracted to everybody of the opposite sex and you have many platonic friendships; the same is true for those who identify as LGBTQ+.
- Be mindful of gender stereotypes in your home and family and try to avoid them as much as possible. This could be in what you say, phrases you use, toys you buy and so on. If friends or relatives keep sending highly gender-stereotyped cards or gifts, gently ask them to stop doing so and suggest what they may consider instead.
- Allow and encourage your tween to have freedom over their own appearance. For instance, give them as much autonomy as possible with their hairstyle and their clothing, regardless of their sex.

When I was writing this book, I spoke to some members of the LGBTQ+ community about their feelings growing up, and specifically what they wished their parents had known, or done differently, at the time. While many of these stories relate to events that actually happened when the individuals were in their teens, the actions and words of their parents and carers had clearly already impacted them when they were still in their tween years. I think their stories can help us all to understand how important acceptance, open and honest discussion, mindful communication and, above all, unconditional love are for our LGBTQ+ tweens.

I first thought I liked girls when I was around eight years old and I told my mum that I thought I loved my friend. She told me that we could talk about it when I was older. I didn't understand that I liked both sexes until I developed crushes on boys much later, around thirteen. I was very confused for a long time as I knew I was 'supposed' to like boys. I couldn't understand a lot of it, and then all my understanding came from things I overheard on TV. I didn't come out until I was seventeen because I was embarrassed, ashamed and scared. I always knew my mum would support me, but I was scared about how my sister would react. She had been openly homophobic in the house and not been challenged by my mum. My dad had made homophobic remarks about men, so I assumed that was a no-go area, too. I wish they had known how aware I was of the things they did (and didn't) say around me, and how little things like talking about different families explicitly, or commenting on the news, or calling things out in front of me would have shown me their views and shown me I was safe. I wish they knew that for all the things they avoided telling me, because they didn't have the confidence or thought I was too young, I filled in the gaps from TV, the internet and things kids said at school.

As soon as I had a language for 'crushes' and 'fancying' I noticed that I was a bit different from my friends, in that I fancied the same gender, when I was about seven years old. My not coming out to myself was mainly caused by feeling that it was abnormal and generally stigmatised by peers. I felt mainly confused and quite ashamed – then almost annoyed that of all people, it had happened to me. I really wish one of my parents had been outwardly pro-gay and LGBT+, and that they'd used words like gay and other sexualities such as bisexual and pansexual more often so that it felt more normalised.

I probably knew when I was quite young. It was quite a journey, because you first have to accept it within yourself before you even think about telling other people, and as someone from quite a sheltered Catholic background it felt like I was doing something wrong. But these feelings got a lot easier the more I told people and the more accepting people were. I wish my parents had been more open about the diversity that exists in the world. There is also an issue with stereotypes – for example, my girlfriend's mum reacted by saying, 'You're not going to cut your hair and get tattoos, are you?' Another thing is parents avoiding bringing up relationships and asking if we're seeing anyone, just as they would for their straight child. I found that where my mum would ask my sister if she'd met any nice boys, with me she wouldn't bring it up. I think this was because she didn't quite feel comfortable with it yet.

I personally didn't have the best coming-out experience, although it could have been a lot worse. Everyone apart from my mum was great. Even my nana was fine and said she just wanted me to be happy. My mum was very cautious and aware of how other people would treat me and she never really told me she was OK with it. She kept asking if I was sure; she told me not to tell other people in case I changed my mind, and she even got me to ask the doctor if my feelings could be hormone related and not because of the fact that I was actually just gay. I think a lot of it came from a place of wanting to protect me from people, but she also didn't realise how much the world has improved with LGBT acceptance since she was my age. I think my perfect response would have just been for her to say that she accepted me, and that if anyone said anything bad, we would take them on together.

I think I knew I was gay in primary school. It felt different to not want girlfriends like other boys and I suppose that shapes you when you don't see gay families represented anywhere, so you don't know that will happen for you. I'm under no illusion that my parents didn't know, but it wasn't spoken about at all – not until I brought a boyfriend home at fifteen. And I guess that was my 'coming-out' moment, although with a relatively accepting family I didn't feel the need to formally come out. I wish at the time there was more representation in media which wasn't so 'obvious'. We had *Will & Grace*, *Queer as Folk*, *Ugly Betty*, etc., but the other boys didn't watch that and being interested in those shows just outed you, basically. I wish I could undo some of their silence over my obvious sexuality, to know their opinions and understand their feelings, as well as possibly have just been able to speak about it. Gay people of my age now have created new families of people who understand and support them – people to talk to about sex, relationships and life – and those connections wouldn't just disappear if we had more communicative families, but it would supplement it.

I was obsessed with a female teacher around the age of seven or eight, and the boys I had posters of as a pre-teen were all gay, but I had no understanding of this at that age. I had lots of boyfriends, but I never felt any connection with them and I didn't know any different. I then got a new group of friends around the age of twelve and met an older lesbian and instantly became infatuated with her. I had a boyfriend at the time, and again, it took me a while to realise what the feelings were that I felt towards this girl. I then kissed a girl for the first time at age thirteen and felt instant connection. I went to an all-girls school, so faced some issues around girls not wanting to change around me for PE. I felt quite confused by it all and I came out to my dad; he was very angry and said it was just a phase. This led to more confusion and mistrust between us and me becoming very closed off. My dad's response made me question if I was just going through a phase, and he would say I was doing it for attention; this then made me second-guess myself, which was very difficult when being confused around sexuality anyway!

I wish my dad had known that I could still have a loving relationship and have children and be happily married. When I came out to my mum she really questioned if I was sure as she said I was going to make life very hard for myself. I wish my parents had been open to discussing how I felt about different relationships I had and how different relationships made me feel, to help me distinguish my feelings earlier on. We were never open to discussing personal relationships or feelings and I wish we had had that open dialogue and to have been told that any feelings are OK and they can be confusing to start with and sometimes they can take a while to become clear.

What if your tween identifies as transgender?

Again, your tween needs unconditional love and acceptance from you. They need you to support them, to be guided by them and respect their needs and to stand up and be an advocate for them. Once again, open-minded communication and approachability are key. Find a supportive, trustworthy and confidential source of information and advice, and gain support away from your tween. You will understandably have lots of big emotions of your own, but your tween needs your home – and you – to be a safe harbour, which means they need strength from you. They will also, ideally, need their own safe space to gain support and research away from you, too. You will find some support organisations listed in the Resources section (see page 243), and you may also consider making an appointment to see your family doctor and requesting a referral to a gender identity development service (GIDS). Seeking professional support and advice is important, whether your tween is sure they are transgender or if they may just be gender questioning (support is not only for those who are definitely trans).

Ask your child if they would like you to change the way you speak to them – with different pronouns, perhaps, or a different name – and respect their requests (see the box below).

Finally, don't make assumptions about your tween's sexuality if they identify as transgender. Gender and sexual attraction are two different things, so the points mentioned earlier about being inclusive with language over future romantic partners is still important.

GENDER PRONOUNS

Most people tend to use the words 'she' and 'he' to refer to themselves, while individuals who are transgender and non-binary often prefer different pronouns. The most common ones include:

- she/her
- he/him
- they/them
- ze/zir.

The last two pairs are gender neutral and may be used to replace she/her and he/him as follows:

- '*They* are going to drama club after school today.'
- 'I had a lovely day with *them* at the park today.'
- '*Ze* loves to bake cakes.'
- 'I went swimming with *zir* today.'

Teaching body autonomy and consent

I've always been a huge advocate of body autonomy (the right for an individual to have control over what is, or isn't, done to their own body) in the early years, encouraging parents to ask their baby or toddler's permission before touching them. Many are confused by this and ask, 'Why would you ever ask your baby permission to change their nappy?' It may seem strange, especially when the baby can't answer you, but importantly, it helps parents to respect their child's body autonomy right from the start. I am also a strong advocate of not forcing children to give relatives or family friends a kiss or hug to say goodbye at the end of a visit. Once again, respecting the child's wishes and not forcing them to make intimate bodily contact with somebody they don't want to touch sets the foundations for the years ahead.

Body autonomy starts at home, with the way you treat your

children. The natural follow on from this is that they expect the same treatment from others. Your one goal when it comes to encouraging your tween to have body autonomy is to teach them that they can say 'No' and that they do not have to do anything with their body that they do not want to do, or allow anybody to touch them in a way that they do not want. It doesn't matter what area of their body is involved, they have the power to say 'Stop touching me, I don't like it', whether somebody is trying to hold their hand or trying to touch their genitals. Speaking of the latter, I strongly recommend teaching your child the 'PANTS Rule', developed by the National Society for Prevention of Cruelty to Children (NSPCC). PANTS stands for:

- Privates are private.
- Always remember your body belongs to you.
- No means no.
- Talk about secrets that upset you.
- Speak up, someone can help.

You can find further information about teaching the PANTS rule in the Resources section (see page 243). Do remember, though, that body autonomy applies to any part of the body and to anybody touching your tween, including you. So once again, if you don't already, try to get into the habit of asking your tween's permission before touching them and don't ever force them to kiss or hug a friend or relative. It's not rude, it's respectful. Encourage them to give them a high five, a fist bump or a special wave instead.

Having 'the sex talk'

Talking to your child about 'the birds and the bees' is a conversation that ideally needs to happen well before the tween years.

Openness and honesty from an early age is the best approach, answering questions as they naturally occur, rather than sitting down and having a specific talk. However, I'm well aware that as a parent this can feel awkward, and many postpone the conversation, so that before they know it, their child is approaching puberty and they realise they haven't had 'the talk' yet.

First off, if you haven't been open with your tween from a young age and haven't discussed sex with them yet, don't worry – it's very much a case of better late than never, because if you don't have a conversation with your child, they will learn from friends, TV, books, magazines and the internet, where you are unable to control the messages that they receive. The following tips can help:

- Try to have several smaller talks, rather than sitting them down for one big one; this can make things easier for both of you and also gives them time to absorb information and come back to you with more questions.
- Pick a natural time for conversation, rather than making it a formal occasion. This works well if you are talking about something together that could organically lead into a conversation about sex and relationships.
- Aim to empower them, not scare them, or put them off the idea.
- Never, ever assume that your child is heterosexual or cisgender (see the LGBTQ+ section earlier in this chapter). Talk about sex in diverse relationships.
- Even if you know that school will soon be covering sex and relationships, get in there first. Sadly, a lot of sex, relationship and puberty education at school (sometimes known as PSHE – or personal, social, health and economic education) is of quite poor quality, often delivered by teachers without any specialist training in how to cover the subjects.

- Use books and pamphlets to help but add to these with conversation. Don't just give your child a book and leave them to it.
- Answer questions as honestly as you can and try to work on any discomfort you may be feeling; you don't want to pass on a sense of anxiety to your tween.
- Use the correct anatomical names for parts of the body and simple, straightforward medical terms and explanations to describe what happens to the body during puberty, sex and conception. If you're questioning the best way to explain something to your tween, I find that simply and honestly always works.
- Talk about the emotional aspects of relationships and dating, not just the physical side.
- Speak to them about consent. Not just that they can say 'No' whenever they want to, but also making sure that the other person is enjoying it and wants to continue, too.
- Make sure your tween knows that they can ask you any questions, whenever they want. Some may prefer to have a little book that they can write notes to you in. You can then write an answer back. Just ask them what their preference is.

Once again, a lot of tween parenting comes back to our own childhoods and feelings around certain subjects. Many people find it hard to talk about sex to their tweens because their parents weren't open with them about it when they were young. You have a wonderful opportunity to break the cycle of embarrassment and communication difficulties with your tween and, in turn, your future grandchildren, too.

I hope this chapter has helped to give you some insight into current issues surrounding love, relationships and gender and how they relate to tweens. Sometimes all the information can feel a little overwhelming, particularly with how quickly LGBTQ+ terminology seems to move for those who don't consider themselves to be LGBTQ+. However, I think it's important for parents and carers to embrace the wonderfully diverse world we live in and the fact that we can help to make the next generation the most accepting and emotionally literate one ever – a generation for whom all love is welcome, regardless of sex or gender, and where individuals all know what a positive relationship feels like and how they deserve to be treated. This is a good point at which to end this chapter and move on to the next, which is all about tweens feeling comfortable in their own bodies.

Chapter 7

Encouraging Body Positivity in the Tween Years

'What is fundamentally beautiful is compassion, for yourself and those around you. That kind of beauty enflames the heart and enchants the soul.'

LUPITA NYONG'O, actor and author

I was still at junior school the first time I went on a diet. I had no need to – I wasn't overweight. But in my head, I had convinced myself I was. I didn't look like the models in the magazines my mum read, or like the pop stars I watched on TV, although it wasn't this comparison that triggered me to restrict what I ate. I didn't do that until my mother joined a slimming group (I'm almost certain she didn't need to). Suddenly, she began counting the calories in everything, weighing the food she ate even more than she weighed her body. One week, she came home from her diet club with a 'Slimmer of the week' award and I still remember how proud she was of it – as if losing weight was the best thing she had achieved for years. I didn't realise at the time how impactful her behaviour was on me. I started to count calories, too, as my mum's slimming recipe books and photocopied diet-plan pamphlets were always to hand in our kitchen. I spent hours poring over them, and by the age of ten, I could probably have told you the calorie content of almost all foods.

The day I started to diet was the day I lost control of my eating, beginning a lifetime of struggling with my weight – ironic, considering I barely weighed 8 stone when I started. I still wonder what my relationship with food and my body would have been like through my tween and teen and, later, adult years if my mum hadn't joined that slimming group.

Body image becomes a huge deal for many in the tween years. Research indicates that tweens start to have negative feelings about their bodies and consider, or even start, dieting from as young as six years old.[1] Changing bodies, as puberty starts, can trigger some children, especially girls, to believe that they are overweight, even if they aren't, and although tween girls show more lowered body confidence and signs of disordered eating than boys, they are not immune either.[2] We live in a society that values thinness and rejects bodies that are deemed to have too much fat. Our girls are bombarded with images of unnaturally thin models, TV and film stars and social-media influencers (often peddling diet products) and our boys receive the subliminal message that the only male body valued and desired is that which is 'ripped', with a clearly defined six-pack and bulging biceps.

Negative influences are everywhere, but mothers have a particular impact on their tweens' (particularly their daughters') body image and dieting behaviour. The more a mother fixates on her own weight and talks negatively about her own body, the more likely her daughter is to do the same.[3]

This chapter introduces some of the ways in which parents can raise their tweens to avoid the diet and low-body-image trap that so many fall into. And while we're on the subject of tweens valuing their bodies, we will also revisit the idea of autonomy – this time focusing on tweens having ownership of their own bodies and how they choose to decorate them.

Nurturing a positive body image in tweens

Being more mindful of your own language and actions, as well as specific actions and words that can help your tween's self-love, is the perfect blend for raising a body-positive, diet-proof tween:

- Help your tween to realise that all bodies are beautiful. Beauty doesn't mean thin, or muscular, it means somebody who is happy in their skin and who celebrates their unique individuality. Make sure that you don't comment negatively when you see someone who is large, or praise somebody for weight loss or their thin frame in your tween's presence.

- Try to not to praise your tween for their looks, or rather their bodies; avoid saying things like, 'Wow, your waist looks tiny in that' or, 'That shirt really shows off your muscles.'

- Help your tween to see that they are so much more than just their appearance. They are their personalities, their hobbies and interests, their friends, their place in your family, the subjects they enjoy at school ... Their body is just one tiny element of who they are.

- Surround your tween with good examples of body positivity. These could be in the form of photos or inspirational quotes hung in your home, a coffee-table book that celebrates difference, a TV programme or a film you watch together.

- Focus on the power of the body and what it can achieve. Speak about athletes and how strong they are, how fast they can run and their endurance.

- Model gratefulness for your own body in front of your tweens. If you've just been for a long walk together, you could say, for example, 'My legs are tired, but they've done such a lot of work. I'm really grateful for them.'

- Help your tween to spot unrealistic portrayals of bodies – say, by talking about how Photoshop manipulates images.
- If you buy your tween books or magazines, try to choose ones with positive role models who have strong personality traits and abilities, rather than a fixation on their bodies and looks.
- If your tween uses social media, try to make sure they follow influencers who are body positive, and who celebrate bodies of all shapes, sizes and colours.
- Encourage a love of exercise, but not with the aim of burning calories or losing fat; instead, emphasise the enjoyment and fun of moving your body with things like cycling, trampolining, dancing, swimming and climbing.
- Never comment about your own appearance negatively around your tween, especially your weight or body shape or size. Remember, what you say and think about your body is highly likely to become what your tween thinks about their own.

It's probably obvious from the above list that a lot of the work needed to raise a tween with a positive body image involves working on your own thoughts and feelings. Although this can seem daunting, especially if you don't have a good relationship with your own body, try to see it as an opportunity not only to raise a body-positive tween but also to change your own relationship with your body to something far better.

What if your tween is overweight?

As your tween's body changes from a child's to one that is beginning to resemble an adult's, it can be hard not to worry about their new curves. It seems quite common for tweens to temporarily carry a little extra weight as they go through puberty, but rather than jumping in and trying to restrict what they eat – or, indeed, putting them on a diet – your best approach would be to rein in the control, take all focus off of their appearance, offer a healthy range of foods and follow the body positivity tips above.

Research consistently finds that when parents attempt to control their child's eating, the child is more likely to be overweight, not only in their tween and teen years, but in adulthood, too.[4] The more parents or carers restrict food, or impose a diet, the more weight the child is likely to gain. Scientists have found that when parents place firm boundaries on eating, children are likely to eat more – not only when they're hungry but also when they are not.[5] Further research has also found that when parents stop their children eating snacks, or what they may term 'junk food', the children eat significantly more of the prohibited foods when they are allowed access to them and desire them more in their absence, which is the perfect recipe for creating a binge-eating problem.[6] In short, the more you restrict so-called 'unhealthy' foods, the more your tween will crave them and have poor control around them when they do have access.

So what should you do if your child is overweight? Aside from providing a wide range of nutritious foods, offered with no pressure, focus on teaching your child how to eat mindfully. By this I mean teaching them about hunger and satiety and being aware of the cues their bodies give them. Encourage them to notice when they are full, so they can stop eating and teach them to ask themselves, 'Am I really hungry right now?' before they reach for a snack. This prevents eating out of comfort or boredom. If they are hungry, help them to make good choices. For instance, it may be easy to grab a chocolate bar, but a slice of toast is more likely to fill them up. Alongside this, try to encourage your tween to move more, not in a workout sort of way, but in a way that they enjoy. Even better is if it's done as a family, going for bike rides together at the weekend, a swimming session together at your local pool or a family game of football at your local park. The emphasis here should always be on fun, family time and enjoyment, not losing weight (so be careful not to mention how many calories they are burning, or how good the activity is for losing weight).

Junk-food addiction

The tween years usually mean an increased intake of sugary and fast foods, with research showing significantly more sugar consumed by tweens than in their earlier childhood years.[7] This increase is likely due to increasing levels of independence, such as shopping and socialising with friends, and more free choice over meals during the day once they start high school. Potentially, this increased intake of so-called junk food could also be due to its having previously been restricted. Once tweens are let off the leash a little, they finally get their fill of all the foods that were banned when they were younger. The answer to this is much the same as above – try to relinquish control. The tighter you hold the reins, the more likely your tween is to binge on sugary and fatty fast food in your absence. Research has shown that restricting sweets and sugary food leads tweens to focus more of their attention on trying to obtain them.[8]

Scientists have also found that 97 per cent of teenage boys say that they eat 'fast food' occasionally, with 14 per cent admitting to eating it every day.[9] First, we must consider our own influence as parents. In part, this is due to the example we set: if we regularly eat junk food ourselves, our children are going to copy us; and, once again, if we avoid it and overly restrict it, then they are more likely to seek it out. The free availability of junk food and a tween's proximity to it impacts, too. Tweens and teens are more likely to buy junk food if they pass an outlet on their way to or from school, or if they have seen adverts for the retailer.[10] Research has shown just how influential advertising is when it comes to fast-food outlets, with adverts hugely improving brand recognition in teens.[11] Influential adverts aren't just limited to TV and cinema screenings though: social-media advertising from junk-food brands targeted at teens shows a good response and interaction from the children targeted.[12]

Emotions can – and do – influence what tweens eat, and how much. Fast and sugary foods have been linked to emotions and a child's ability to regulate them.[13] In other words, tweens eat more junk when they're feeling down or dysregulated emotionally, with sugary and carbohydrate-heavy foods producing a dopamine high, which helps tweens to manage stress. Once again, we need to help our tweens to eat intuitively – to focus on eating only when hungry and stopping when satiated. Alongside this, using some of the methods to cope with big emotions (see page 121) can really help to reduce emotional eating.

Explaining the diet industry and the influencer effect

Tween girls are particularly at risk of being on the receiving end of damaging words and imagery on the internet, especially on social media. Often, these messages are highly sexualised, as well as presenting body ideals and goals that are unrealistic. Research studying nine-year-old girls found their exposure to sexualised media online is linked to them internalising these sexualised messages, believing that they need to 'look sexy' and have 'a sexy body'.[14] Tween girls today are bombarded with these unhealthy messages more than any other generation. And we still don't know what the longer-term effects will be.

Tweens, especially girls, are also surrounded by unhealthy messages from social-media influencers advertising diet products. Of course, boys are not immune to this either. Instagram is arguably one of the worst networks when it comes to this toxic promotion of body ideals. Research has shown that 49 per cent of users who follow accounts described as promoting healthy living and eating display some symptoms of an eating disorder.[15]

How do we help our tweens to see through the social-media messages?

First, be careful about what your tween accesses online. If they do use social media (and do remember most have a minimum age of thirteen for users), keep an eye on who they follow. Make sure your tween knows that most influencers are paid to advertise brands and very rarely are they recommending products that they use personally. Similarly, you should explain that it is an influencer's job to deceive: to present their lives and bodies as perfectly as possible. This involves special lighting, editing software such as Photoshop, carefully thought-out staging and lots of work behind the scenes. They don't wake up looking like that, and away from the cameras and the heavily filtered photos, they look vastly different.

Clothing and hair autonomy

Another important way to increase your tween's body positivity and self-esteem is to give them autonomy over what they wear and how they express themselves via their appearance.

The tween years are very much a transition period: at the start you, the parent or carer, are usually in control of choosing and buying all their clothes and shoes, as well as dictating their haircuts and hairstyles. Towards the end of the tween years, and during the teens, it is important for the child to take more control. This can be hard for parents, particularly if your tween insists on following highly gender-stereotyped styles when you have worked hard to avoid them, or, indeed, if they choose to express themselves by rejecting gender stereotypes, having grown up wearing lots of pretty dresses or so-called 'boyish clothes'. I remember the sadness I felt when my daughter started shunning anything with a floral pattern or a bright colour during her mid-tweens. Instead, she only wore black. In a way, it was almost like a strange sense of grieving, as the change in clothing taste also marked the end of her childhood and the start of adolescence. My feelings were my feelings, though, and I tried hard not to share them with her.

It's so important that tweens are allowed to work out who they are and how they want to be, and their clothing and hairstyles are very much a part of that. This is a time to let go and pass the control on to them. Let them wear what they want, regardless of how you feel about it. Similarly, my sons all had beautiful thick, curly hair that I kept at shoulder length throughout their early years. We were often stopped by strangers in the street who would comment on their angelic, long, curly locks. As they entered their tween years, they all expressed a desire to cut their hair short. I was heartbroken seeing their shorn ringlets on the floor of the hairdresser's; to me, they seemed to symbolise the cutting away of their babyhoods. But, as attached to their hair as I was, it wasn't my hair, and therefore it shouldn't have been my decision to cut it or not.

The following quote from Jada Pinkett Smith – in reply to the question 'Why did you let Willow [her daughter, then aged eleven] cut her hair short?' – summarises everything I aimed for:

The question why I would *let* Willow cut her hair. First the *let* must be challenged. This is a world where women, girls, are constantly reminded that they don't belong to themselves; that their bodies are not their own, nor their power, or self-determination. I made a promise to endow my little girl with the power to always know that her body, spirit, and her mind are her domain. Willow cut her hair, because her beauty, her value, her worth is not measured by the length of her hair. It's also a statement that claims that even little girls have the right to own themselves and should not be a slave to even their mother's deepest insecurities, hopes and desires. Even little girls should not be slaves to the preconceived ideas of what a culture believes a little girl should be.

On a similar note, my daughter asked to have her ears pierced when she was eight years old. I instantly replied, 'No, you're too young.' I would have much preferred her to wait until she was older, preferably until her early teens. After some introspection on my behalf though, I changed my mind. What was really stopping me from allowing her? Was it my personal preferences about children and pierced ears? Or was it because I felt she wasn't old enough to make an informed choice? I realised that at eight, she was mature enough to understand that the piercing would hurt and could carry a risk of infection. We spoke about how scrupulously clean she would have the keep them. She said she would, and I believed her. This brought me to the realisation that actually this had now become much more about me than her. She did understand the risks and repercussions fully and she still wanted it done. Her ears were her ears, not mine. I felt that I had taken on a caretaker role of protecting her body until she could protect it herself, but now was perhaps the right time to start handing over some of that role to her. By preventing her from piercing her ears, I was no longer protecting her body autonomy – I was preventing it. I thought of the Jada Pinkett Smith quote above and booked the appointment for her. She didn't flinch during the piercing and kept her ears immaculately clean afterwards. Her pierced ears brought her a huge sense of joy for months afterwards and I was pleased that I had allowed her the opportunity to make her own informed decision about the care and keeping of her own body.

Allowing tweens to be the caretakers of their own bodies is a good place to end this chapter, while the next one picks up on this idea with a focus on personal hygiene and body care – two things tweens are not well known for!

Chapter 8

Personal Hygiene, Body Care and First Periods

'People often say that motivation doesn't last. Well, neither does bathing – that's why we recommend it daily.'

ZIG ZIGLAR, author

Not so long ago you would hold your newborn son or daughter in your arms, stroking their peachy, soft skin and inhaling the intoxicating scent of baby hair; fast-forward a few years and now you catch a whiff of smelly feet when trainers that are rapidly approaching the same size as yours are abandoned haphazardly by the front door, or you notice that your tween has suddenly developed some big, angry red spots.

Puberty brings with it some unpleasant smells and aesthetics. Alongside preparing our tweens emotionally for what they are – or soon will be – going through, we should also prepare them to take care of their bodies. In previous chapters, we've focused on helping tweens emotionally; this chapter covers priming them for the blood and sweat, as well as the tears. We'll cover how to talk to your tween about body hygiene in a way that actually encourages them to wash regularly, and look at how to cope with acne, body hair and their first visit to an orthodontist. Later, we will look at preparing tweens for their first period and first bra and navigating the maze of respecting your tween's privacy as they grow. Last, but by no means least, we will examine sleep in the tween years and how to make sure your child gets enough.

Smelly bodies

Body odour usually starts to occur between the ages of seven and ten years, with girls commonly experiencing it earlier than boys. Good body hygiene therefore becomes increasingly important in the tween years, for the child's own sake, as well as those living with them. Many parents struggle with tweens avoiding showers and baths. This is often just a symptom of the immature tween brain; as adults, we remember why we need to clean ourselves daily and fully understand the implications of scrimping on personal hygiene – but remember, tweens don't think like us.

You may feel that there is something wrong with your tween, or indeed your parenting, if you must remind them to wash daily, but this is incredibly common and totally normal. The two things I have found to be the most helpful in encouraging daily washing are:

1. Explaining to tweens what causes body odour (stale sweat and bacteria – showing them photographs of what is lurking on their unwashed skin can be powerful) and the repercussions of not washing daily i.e. smelling bad and impacting how others view them (this is a great way to use peer pressure to your advantage!).
2. Creating a form of visual reminder for them – this can be as simple as a sheet of paper pointing out what the tween needs to do each morning, like this:

Remember:

wake up →► brush teeth →► shower →► get dressed →► eat breakfast

Hang this reminder on the back of their bedroom door, or the bathroom door or any other location where they will see it clearly each morning.

I also find that allowing tweens control over the products they use in the shower or bath can make them much more inclined to use them.

Most parents buy their child's first deodorant in the tween years. There is no right or wrong time – rather when you and your tween feel is best (but definitely once they start to get body odour). The following tips can help you to choose a tween-friendly one:

- Check the label carefully. Deodorant aims to eliminate odours, but does not reduce sweat, whereas anti-perspirant reduces sweat and thus odour. Some products perform both functions. Anti-perspirants are generally more effective since they reduce the cause of the odour.
- Ask your tween if they would prefer a roll-on, stick or spray, but be aware that some schools may request that no sprays are used in changing rooms – and if your tween does enjoy spraying and squirting things playfully, it might be an idea to go with a roll-on or stick, so as to avoid adding anything else to their arsenal.
- Consider more natural brands that are aluminium and paraben free for delicate skin.
- Look for eco-conscious brands and ones that use recyclable packaging, such as the natural-rock deodorants or balms in glass jars.

- Do encourage your tween to choose their own deodorant, particularly the scent, where possible. They are much more likely to wear something that they like.

Finally, don't presume that your tween knows how to use their deodorant. I made this mistake with one of my tweens and wondered why he still smelled bad after getting through several cans of deodorant. Upon questioning him, I found that he had been spraying it liberally over his clothes after getting dressed each morning, and not onto his skin.

Spots

Most young people between the ages of ten and twenty will experience acne. However, it's also common for spots to develop between the ages of eight and ten, sometimes even as soon as seven, with earlier onset being more common in girls.

As puberty approaches, rising hormone levels stimulate the sebaceous glands in the skin to secrete more sebum, an oily and waxy substance that can clog the pores. These clogged pores become inflamed, and spots, or acne, form as a result. The most common site of spots in puberty is the face, but it's not uncommon for them to appear on the back and chest, too. If your tween's acne is mild, then the following self-care tips at home can be helpful:

- Clean the skin morning and night only. More frequent washing can encourage more sebum to be produced, which can worsen things.
- Use a mild cleanser, or one specially created for teen skin, avoiding those which are more drying and harsher, which may exacerbate the problem. If using water, make sure the water is not too hot or cold. Body temperature is best.

- Try to choose non-comodogenic (non-clogging) suncreams and moisturisers (and make-up if your tween uses it).
- Keep hair away from the forehead as much as possible, especially if it also tends to be oily.
- Teach your tween to avoid touching their face. This includes not squeezing spots, as this can encourage more oil production and introduce bacteria which can worsen the situation. Squeezing can also lead to permanent scarring.
- Use a gentle exfoliator once a week, to help remove dead skin cells and unclog pores.
- Look into products containing salicylic and glycolic acid. These often come in the form of pre-soaked pads and can help to dissolve some of the dead cells that cause clogging.
- Follow a good, basic, consistent skincare regime. Don't keep swapping and changing products, trying 'the next big thing' in the skincare industry.
- Watch their diet. Try to ensure it is as healthy as possible and that they are getting enough zinc, vitamins A and E and omega-3 fatty acids. Deficiencies of these can exacerbate acne.

If your tween's acne seems to be worsening, especially if they are finding it stressful, then it can be a good idea to visit a dermatologist (a doctor specialising in skincare). They will be able to give expert advice and access to products that may help.

While some tweens are not bothered about acne, for others it can be a cause of great anxiety. Sadly, there are no easy solutions here, but listening to your tween's concerns and providing empathic support should underpin your approach. If you feel that they might benefit from some professional mental-health input, your family doctor should be able to refer you to an individual or organisation best placed to help.

Braces

Once your tween has all of their adult teeth, usually between the ages of eight and eleven, your dentist may refer you to an orthodontist if they believe that their jaw or teeth, or both, are misaligned or overcrowded. It is also possible to self-refer your tween privately (i.e. for a service that you pay for) if their case does not fall into the free treatment category, or if you would rather bypass the long waiting lists and your funds stretch.

After an examination and having taken X-rays and photographs of your tween's mouth, the orthodontist will recommend a specific type of treatment and duration. The most common type of brace is a metal fixed one, sometimes called a traditional brace, or more commonly known as 'train tracks'. This brace has metal brackets fixed to each individual tooth, with a long piece of wire running between them, usually on the top and bottom teeth. The wire places pressure on the teeth, moving them into line. Sometimes tiny rubber bands are hooked onto the brackets to gently pull the jaw into line too. If you are paying for treatment privately, you can opt for so-called 'invisible braces' which have clear or white ceramic brackets. Fixed braces usually stay on for around two years, although sometimes twelve to eighteen months may be enough if the alignment is not too problematic.

Once the fixed brace is removed, the tween (or teen as they will likely be by this time) will usually be fitted with a retainer. This is a plastic moulding of their teeth (a little like a rugby mouth guard), which they wear in the evenings and overnight to hold their teeth in their new position while the jaw continues to grow.

The following tips can help to prepare your tween for their first brace fitting:

- Watch videos online beforehand, so they know what to expect.
- Buy some special cleaning products – such as little brushes that fit under the brace wire – to help your tween to keep their teeth clean. It's also a good idea to get some dental disclosing tablets (tablets they chew which stain plaque on the teeth a purple colour temporarily), so they can see any spots they miss when brushing.
- Stock up on soft or liquid foods that they do not need to chew for the first few days after the fitting. Teeth and jaws can be very painful for two to five days after fitting and tightening appointments.
- Give them some analgesic tablets before any pain comes on. It's easier to control any pain from the beginning, rather than waiting for it to get bad before giving anything.
- Get some dental wax that can be put on the brackets for the first few days to stop them rubbing on the inside of the lips.
- Buy some special gel for mouth ulcers in advance. Tweens can use this to rub on their lips or the inside of their mouth if any sore spots occur.
- Don't plan any big events for the first week following a brace being fitted. It can be extremely uncomfortable and takes time to get used to wearing one.

I would also strongly recommend taking a picture of your child's teeth before their first braces are on, so that you can look back at it once treatment ends. The results of wearing braces are remarkable, and you may not really appreciate how huge the change is until you look back at old photos.

Body hair

As puberty progresses, there is strong pressure from society for girls to have skin that is soft and hairless. We must remember that the growth of hair on the legs, under the arms, on the upper lip and pubic area is normal for our species and not something that is inherently ugly that must be removed. Hairless skin is not somehow more feminine, just as hairy skin is not more masculine, despite what society would have us believe. As with so many other things, it's worth looking at the example you are setting yourself. Do you remove your body hair? Do you make unpleasant comments if you see a woman who doesn't? Tween girls notice what you do, and they notice what you say about others, even if you don't comment on their own developing body hair.

Our goal as parents and carers should be to raise children who are comfortable in their own skins and that includes the hair that grows on them. Boys are not excluded from this either. If your tween seems happy with their body hair, then try to respect that, rather than imposing any views that you may have about its removal; but if they are unhappy with it and you have already spoken to them about societal pressure and stereotypes, then I'm of the firm belief that they should be supported to remove their unwanted hair, if that is what they genuinely want to do. I have come across too many comments online where parents have said, 'My daughter wants to shave her legs, but I think she's too young, so I've told her she has to wait until she's older.' If you don't help your tween to find an effective – and, most importantly, safe – method of hair removal, they will take matters into their own hands. Far better to support them than to find they have cut themselves on a blunt razor they found in the bin while trying to teach themselves to shave their own legs. Once I was certain my daughter wanted to remove her body hair, we visited a local chemist and looked at the various products available. She chose to use a hair-removal cream, as she thought it would be easier for her to use, although we also bought some safety razors and shaving foam in case she wanted to try shaving. I also offered for her to have them waxed by a local beautician, but she wasn't keen on the pain, no matter how fleeting. Each of my boys had their own safety razor when they expressed an interest in shaving and my husband took some time to teach them how to use it safely and effectively. A good alternative is to find some online instruction videos showing how to shave, and to watch them together.

Menarche

When my daughter was in her early tweens, I spent some time making up a 'first period box' for her. I wanted to have everything she needed, ready for her first period (menarche). We had previously had a conversation about the type of sanitary protection she might prefer, including the following options:

- **Cloth sanpro (sanitary protection)** These are sanitary towels made from fabric – usually cotton or bamboo – that are washed (in the washing machine on a regular cycle) and reused after each use. They usually have poppers and 'wings', so they can be easily fixed in place, and they come in lots of cool patterns and colours. While the initial outlay is more expensive than it would be for disposables, you soon save money.
- **Period pants** These are special knickers that have a moisture-wicking-and-retaining lining, meaning that no other protection is needed. They look remarkably like normal underwear and come in a range of sizes and colours. Like cloth sanpro, the initial outlay is expensive, but you save money in the long run. Sometimes they are

used as an added layer of extra protection, like towels or tampons, to prevent 'leakage', which can be particularly useful while at school if your tween has an especially heavy or erratic flow (which is common initially).

- **Menstrual cups** Soft cups, usually made from silicone or latex, these are inserted into the vagina and collect menstrual blood. They need to be regularly emptied but can be washed and reinserted. They are usually cheap to buy.
- **Regular sanitary towels** These are the disposable stick-on towels that most are familiar with, although you can buy special tween/teen-sized ones. Many of the main companies will send free samples if you request them on their websites, so your tween can find the one they are most comfortable with.
- **Tampons** Again, one of the two most mainstream choices, alongside regular sanitary towels. Here, your tween can choose between a tampon that comes with an applicator (a special tube that can make insertion easier) or a non-applicator type, where the tampon has to be inserted with the fingers. Once again, most of the well-known manufacturers offer free samples on their websites.

Although several companies sell 'first period' boxes, I preferred to make my own, not only because it was cheaper, but because I could personalise what I included. Here are some ideas:

- A selection of sanitary protection.
- Some new comfy knickers (including spares to keep in their bag in case of any leaks).
- Some wipes, in case of any accidents and if hand-washing facilities aren't available when changing protection.
- A hot-water bottle or heat pad, in case of discomfort.
- Some snuggly socks ... just because (who doesn't feel more comfortable in soft socks?).

- A couple of bars of favourite chocolate.
- A fun face mask (of the cosmetic, not Covid type).
- Some little motivational quote cards.
- A bottle of favourite bubble bath or shower gel.
- Some herbal or fruity tea bags, or hot chocolate sachets.
- A packet of tissues.
- A small gift – for my daughter, this was some hair ties and her favourite body spray.

I packaged all these things up in a box and gave it to my daughter as soon as I noticed the first signs of puberty. I explained what everything was for and suggested she might want to keep some items in her school bag, just in case her periods began while she was at school. Most importantly though, she had everything ready, which meant that if I was not around when she started, she wouldn't have to try to find whatever she needed herself. This gave her an element of control which I think is useful for young girls when helping them to prepare for their menarche. Some people also write special letters or cards, and some also have a 'coming-of-age' party or ceremony of some sort to celebrate menarche.

First bras

I remember reading *Are You There, God? It's Me, Margaret* by Judy Blume as a tween and becoming a little obsessed with the idea of a first bra. When my mum finally took me for a fitting, in our local Marks and Spencer, I was so disappointed to find that I had absolutely no choice. The only first bra available was a plain, ugly white one. Things have changed dramatically since I was a child and now there is a huge array of first bras to choose from. The plain white ones are still there, but they are accompanied by others in a whole rainbow of colours and styles.

It's now common for tweens to start with soft, unstructured bralettes or crop tops for a couple of years before graduating to their first 'proper' bra, but importantly, there is a huge amount of choice. Most girls are somewhere between the ages of ten and thirteen when they get their first bra, which coincides with breast growth during puberty. As with menarche, I think the best approach is to have the 'when-to-get-a-bra' conversation with tween girls before they need one. I agreed with my daughter that we would make shopping for her first bra a special day, for just the two of us. We would go for a fitting, then a nice lunch and enjoy an afternoon doing whatever she wanted. It became something she looked forward to, rather than something to fear. If you haven't already agreed on what to do and your daughter is already showing breast growth, then the best way forward is to talk to her about when she would like a bra. You could look at some pictures of first bras online and talk about the styles and types she likes best. Ideally, you would go for a professional fitting – specialist lingerie shops would be my first port of call if you have one locally – and do reassure her that she can be measured over her clothes, without being naked in front of a stranger. If you can't get to a store, however, you can find fitting instructions online.

Privacy please

When my children were young, I never seemed to get any privacy away from them. I got used to going to the toilet with at least one child attached to my leg and I rarely had a bath alone. Toddlers often seem happier without clothes on, and all my children would happily run around our house stark naked. But as soon as they entered the tween years, bedroom and bathroom doors would suddenly be closed, and I had to quickly adapt and respect their requests for privacy.

Rising consciousness of changing bodies often means closed doors, even for those tweens who were previously happy to be naked around you. Similarly, some tweens become uncomfortable with their parents being naked around them when they weren't before. Regardless of how you feel about nudity around your children, if your tween expresses concern at you being naked around them, it's best to respect that and close doors yourself. If you have a tween who is happy to be naked in your presence, then once again, the best thing to do is to follow their lead. There really is no right or wrong way to handle nakedness and privacy in the tween years, only the way that is right or wrong for your tween.

Sleep in the tween years

In Chapter 1, we learned about the chronotype shift – the genetic encoding that makes tweens want to go to sleep later at night and get up later in the morning. Your role as a parent or carer in the tween years when it comes to sleep is to ensure your tween gets enough sleep, while being mindful of their changing chronotype. I find the biggest mistake parents of tweens make when it comes to sleep is trying to get them to go to bed too early. This results in the child finding it difficult to get to sleep, lots of arguments and bedtime procrastination. Ultimately, this results in an even later sleep onset time, not earlier.

All tweens have different sleep needs, as do adults, but a good bedtime for this age group – taking into consideration scientific research and biological norms – is around 9 p.m. I would go further, however, and say one hour either side is fine; so a sleep onset time of anywhere between 8 p.m. and 10 p.m. is likely appropriate, with the majority sitting somewhere in the middle.

The following tips can help to improve bedtime and thus, hopefully, allow your tween to get enough sleep at night. You should still expect a certain element of grumpiness though, and a resistance to getting up in the morning. Remember, this is not your tween being lazy, but rather their shifting chronotype making it genuinely hard for them to wake up.

- Try to encourage your tween to have a good, consistent bedtime routine – say, starting with a shower or bath, followed by PJs on and teeth brushing, then reading a book to themselves for twenty minutes or so, before lights off and going to sleep.
- Keep all screens out of the bedroom. Your tween should not be exposed to these (including TVs, laptops and mobiles) for at least an hour before their regular sleep onset time.
- Only use very dim – preferably red – lighting in the bedroom. Red is the only wavelength of light that doesn't negatively affect the secretion of melatonin – the sleep hormone. Most nightlights now have a red option; alternatively, use a colour-changing light bulb set on red. Red fairy-light strings also make great tween-friendly bedroom lighting.
- Never send your tween to their bedroom as a punishment. They need to view their room as a happy, positive, relaxing space, not somewhere associated with exclusion or penalties.
- Try to end the evening with a chat to your tween about their day, to ensure that they don't go to bed with worries on their mind. This is often the time that they will open up to you the most, so you can have more productive talks.
- If your tween struggles to get to sleep, encourage them to listen to a sleep meditation or mindfulness recording.
- Never insinuate your tween is too old to sleep with their teddy, lovey or other comforter. If it provides comfort,

then they still need it. Many adults also need to sleep with a special blanket, pillow or similar.

- Check your tween's diet. Deficiencies in iron, magnesium and omega-3 fatty acids can impact sleep negatively.

Sleep in the tween years is vital, but don't just *tell* your tween it's important. Tweens are much more likely to work on their sleep and go to bed earlier if they understand *why*. Explain to them why it's important, or even better – show them! An article or video about the negative impact of sleep deprivation can be powerful and so much more effective than your constant pleading with them to go to bed.

It's impossible to avoid some of the more unpleasant aspects of puberty completely, but making sure that your tween feels as empowered as possible to tackle whatever hand fate deals them can go a long way to helping their mental health while they are going through the experience. Encouraging tweens to take good care of their bodies now will also stand them in good stead for the adult years ahead.

Chapter 9

How to Raise Tween Allies and Activists

'We showed that we are united and that we, young people, are unstoppable.'

GRETA THUNBERG

I n the summer of 2018, fifteen-year-old Swedish schoolgirl Greta Thunberg stood outside the Swedish parliament holding a sign that read *'Skolstrejk för klimatet'* ('School strike for climate'). Greta was protesting for the government to implement more action on climate change. And what started with one schoolgirl soon spread to other tweens and teens from around the world and a movement known as 'Fridays for Future' began: inspired by Greta, millions of young students would stay off school on Fridays and congregate in public places holding placards calling for adults – and particularly governments – to act. Greta has since spoken at the United Nations Climate Change Conference and the Climate Action Summit and was named *Time* magazine's 'Person of the Year' in 2019 – the youngest individual to ever receive the accolade.

The so-called 'Greta effect' is widespread, with more and more young people standing up for what they believe in. When writing this chapter, I was reminded of the words of anthropologist Margaret Mead: 'Never doubt that a small group of thoughtful, committed citizens can change the world; indeed, it's the only thing that ever has.' There has never been such a pertinent time for our tweens to take a stand on important issues, such as climate change, as well as other causes close to their hearts. Quite simply, this generation is the one who really could change the world for the better. Our tweens can not only grow to be the activists and allies of tomorrow, but, as Greta has shown, their voices carry tremendous impact today, too. To quote the title of Greta's book: 'No one is too small to make a difference.'[1]

In this chapter, we will look at how to raise your tween to be an activist and an ally, no matter what cause they support. First, though, we once again have to start with you. While you yourself don't necessarily have to champion the causes your tween believes in, you do need to check your own biases and make sure you are not passing them on to them. Regardless of how free of prejudices you think you may be, it's likely that you do hold some beliefs or behaviours that illustrate unconscious bias, or at least a lack of understanding and action. Which is why to raise allies and activists we must begin by (re)educating ourselves (see Resources, page 243, for a good place to start).

Teaching tweens the difference between equality and equity

There is much talk in society today of treating everyone fairly and equally. The concept of equality is probably one your tween is already aware of. And while equality seems like a great idea initially, the concept of equity is really what we should all aim for. Equality means to treat all people the same, but what this misses is that sometimes people need to be treated differently:

being mindful of somebody's needs and abilities and how they may differ from others', while being sure that the individual will not be disadvantaged by these differences, is known as equity.

Let's imagine that a group of tweens is sitting an exam at school, with two different scenarios:

- **Scenario one**: all the tweens are treated identically. They have the same amount of time to complete the exam, in the same room, with the same exam paper. This is equality.
- **Scenario two**: the tweens are treated differently, based upon their abilities. Most will sit the exam in the same room, with the same amount of time and the same exam paper. Some who have dyslexia, however, will be given an extra fifteen minutes to complete the exam, their paper will be in larger print and they will be able to take the exam in a smaller, quieter room to enable better concentration. These differences ensure that they have the same chance of exam success as their neurotypical peers. This is equity.

As parents and carers, we must make sure our tweens understand the difference between these two and encourage them to speak up for others if they think that equity has been overlooked in the quest for equality. It is not enough to raise tweens to see everybody equally; they must notice differences to strive for equity.

Understanding the bystander effect

Watch any film or television programme showing a fight among a group of tweens and teens and you will always see a circle of onlookers. Rarely do we see any intervening. Most parents and carers watching these fictional representations will say, 'My child wouldn't do that – they would speak up and try to stop the fight.' Social psychologists would disagree.

For decades, experiments have shown that adults are far less likely to intervene in a difficult or emergency situation if others are present. The more bystanders there are, the less likely it is that one of them will intervene. And conversely, if there are no other bystanders, it is far more likely that somebody will act. This effect is by no means limited to adults, it occurs with tweens and teens, too. The bystander effect is based on two main ideas:

1. **'Diffusion of responsibility'** – where individuals feel that the more witnesses there are, the less personally responsible they are for intervening.
2. **'Social influence'** – which describes how bystanders look to the behaviour of others to gauge how they themselves should act. So if others are not intervening, they believe that they shouldn't either.

The best way to reduce the impact of the bystander effect on your tween is to make sure that they understand the concept. You can do this organically, when a situation occurs – for instance, if you are watching a film together and notice the bystander effect. Teach your tween to be what is known as an upstander: somebody who will stand up for others and speak up about unjust behaviour, regardless of what others are doing. It takes a certain degree of confidence and self-esteem for tweens to act in the opposite way to most of their peers, so the information covered in Chapters 4 and 5 is also important here.

Finally, if you do hear that your tween has intervened and helped, make sure that you praise them for their efforts, especially if they have been overlooked by others (such as their school).

Kindness is not enough

When was the last time you saw a social-media meme, a notebook, a piece of wall art or a T-shirt emblazoned with the words 'Be kind'? Kindness seems to be the buzzword of the moment and has been embraced by marketers everywhere. But kindness should not be the ultimate goal for ourselves or our children.

Kindness implies a degree of passivity, whereby social injustices can be brushed off if you smile and are kind. And while the world would undoubtedly be a better place if everybody was kinder, we need to raise children to take a more active role in changing society. We need them to celebrate, not just accept, differences. We need to raise our tweens to be actively anti-racist, rather than simply 'not racist'; anti-homophobic and anti-transphobic, rather than just 'not homophobic or transphobic'; and anti-sexist, rather than just 'not sexist'. We need to raise allies, who will stand up and speak up for others, not sink into the background with a kind smile. You will find some ways to encourage this below, but remember that to raise allies, you yourself must be actively anti-racist, anti-homophobic, anti-transphobic and a strong feminist and eco-ally. So while these tips may apply to your tween, remember to work on yourself just as much (see Resources, page 243 for more help with this).

How to raise an anti-racist tween

- Make sure that your home shows diversity. Think about the books you buy for yourself, your tween and any siblings. Consider any art hanging on your walls, the music you listen to, the films you watch and the toys you buy.
- Teach your children why black lives matter and why this is different to 'all lives matter'. All lives do matter,

of course, but it is black lives that are currently at risk and therefore need our focus. This does not diminish the value of any other lives.

- Check your own language and that of your family members and friends. If they are racist, pull them up on it, especially when your tween is with you.
- If you don't already do so, show your support by spending money with black-owned businesses.
- Teach your tweens about black history and the history of their own country, particularly those with a colonial past. Don't leave this to their school, as it is rarely covered in any depth (if at all).
- Teach them to be upstanders, to speak up if they see or hear any racism.
- Talk about racism with your tween often. Pick up on stories in the news with them so that they see that racism is very much active today and not just a part of history.

How to raise an anti-homophobic and anti-transphobic tween

- Actively seek out television programmes, books and films with gay or trans main characters and those with diverse relationships and families. (A favourite in our house is the 2018 film *Love, Simon* – a film about a teenage boy who hasn't yet told anybody that he is gay.) Watch them together and comment on how lovely it is to see and celebrate diversity in relationships.
- Speak up about any homophobic or transphobic conversations you may hear when with your tween and pull them up on any language they use, too. Sometimes tweens use terminology without fully understanding what it implies, just because it is commonly used by their peers.

- Consider joining in a local Pride celebration or march with your tween.
- Challenge gender stereotypes when out with your tween. Point out how silly it is that products are labelled for boys or for girls, when they should be embraced by everybody. If you see somebody breaking gender norms, remark on how fantastic it is to see such authenticity.
- Be consistent in your own actions and with your own words. Pick yourself up on any prejudice or stereotyping.

How to raise a feminist tween

- Don't presume that feminism is just for girls. It isn't. It is just as important – if not more so – to raise boys to be feminists.
- Point out common sexist injustices in the world, such as the gender pay gap, and teach your tween about countries where women are treated differently from men and have fewer rights.
- Teach your tween about the suffragette movement and what it means for women (and men) today.
- Be mindful of sexist language – such as dismissing women as 'Karens' or using phrases such as 'man up'. If your tween uses such words or phrases, have a conversation with them about what they mean and how they impact on us and others.
- Watch films and TV programmes with strong female characters, especially ones that avoid gender stereotypes. A favourite in our house was the *Hunger Games* series of books and films; we also love Rey in *Star Wars*.
- Point out gender stereotypes when you are out shopping with your tween, encouraging them to spot their own and discussing how these can harm children, especially

girls, as they grow. For example, toys aimed at boys that promote STEM (science, technology, engineering and maths), compared to toys for girls that focus on looking pretty or raising babies.

Raising an eco-aware tween

- Teach your tween about recycling and encourage them to help sort the family's rubbish and collect other items such as crisp packets and empty glass bottles to take to a central recycling collection point.
- Explain the impact of fast fashion to your tween and encourage them to learn to repair their clothes, customise them or even make their own with your help.
- Visit charity shops and boot sales as a family and discuss how purchasing second-hand is helpful for the environment, as well as being cheaper.
- Talk about the importance of conserving water and reducing your use of gas and electricity in your home and about how their actions (such as remembering to switch off lights when they leave a room) can help. If you have a smart meter, show them how much energy certain things use so they can see the direct impact.
- Encourage them to love nature by spending lots of time in it as a family. Buy a bird-, insect- or tree-spotting book, take part in summer butterfly or back-garden bird counts (often organised by national wildlife charities and local authorities) and, if you have a garden, give them their own section to grow vegetables and flowers.
- Discuss current news stories that cover environmental issues and what actions tweens can take to help to protect the environment.

- Join a local environmental party, or a national charity. Many produce newsletters and booklets for tweens as part of a membership package.

These lists are by no means exhaustive, but they do provide a good starting point. It is most likely that the journey to being anti-racist, anti-homophobic, anti-transphobic, anti-sexist and more eco-aware is one you will also need to take with your tween. Of course, nobody is perfect – but we can all improve, as well as teaching our tweens.

Explaining poverty and social inequality

As children get older, they start to notice the inequality in the world more. I remember the first time my children saw a homeless person on the streets of London, they were confused and didn't understand why he was sleeping in a doorway. As adults, we can become immune to the plight of others, especially if we are fortunate enough not to struggle much ourselves, and we become the bystanders we spoke of earlier in this chapter. If we want our tweens to aim for equity and to treat others with respect, we must explain poverty and social inequality to them from a young age. The following tips can help:

- Explain the common reasons behind homelessness and poverty to children – for example, disability and illness, the income gaps between rich and poor, education inequality and lack of jobs. Help them to see the story behind the person.
- Help your tween to understand that poverty is common and isn't only restricted to the extremes of homelessness. Your tween will have at least one child living in poverty

in their class at school. Explain the effects this may have on the hypothetical classmate – what happens if they go to school hungry?

- Don't avoid tricky questions if your tween asks them. Try to answer them as honestly as possible, with no judgement of the situation somebody may find themselves in. Help your tween to view the other person's position with empathy.
- Speak to your tween about stories on the news, or events that happen locally, pointing out how poverty or social inequality have impacted others.
- You could collect supplies for your local food bank with your tween. Encourage them to find a list of items most in need – these are often available on food banks' websites or social-media pages – and give them a budget to shop for them at your local store. Then place them in the collection bin or drop them off at the local food bank. Some would be happy for your tween to visit to learn more about their activities, too.
- Speak to your tween about their privileges and how these affect their lives, not just now, but in the future – giving them access to good education, for example.
- Encourage your tween to investigate their own causes to support. They might think of a way they could raise money for a local or national charity, say, with a sponsored walk.

Your main goal when speaking about social inequality and poverty with your tween should be to help them respect the individuals affected and view them with empathy, understanding that poverty is something that could affect any one of us at some point in our lives.

Introducing tweens to politics

It may seem an awfully long time until your tween turns eighteen and is old enough to vote, but don't let that put you off teaching them about politics. The way a country is run has a direct impact on our tweens today and dictates a large part of their future, so it seems wrong to avoid conversations about this just because a child is young. I always recommend that parents take their children with them whenever they vote, but this is so much more important in the tween and teen years.

Following on from the topic of raising a feminist (see page 183), making sure you vote in every election has a big influence on your tween. It's a great chance to talk about the suffragettes and why they worked so hard to win women the right to vote, and a perfect moment to talk about democracy and why each and every one of us matters. Even if you are jaded with politics and feel that there is no point casting your vote, the message you send your tween with your action (or inaction) matters. By voting, you show your tween that their voice can be heard and that they should appreciate the actions of those who came before them. As an election approaches, share with your tween any flyers that are posted through your letterbox, encourage them to join you at the front door to ask canvassers questions that are important to them, listen to news reports and debates together and ask your tween who they would vote for. You could even encourage them to talk to their teachers and ask to hold a mock election at school.

Of course, voting isn't the only way your tween can make a difference. As they grow into adulthood, if they feel passionate, they could consider joining a political party, even standing as a candidate themselves. Do be careful not to impose your political views on your child though. Let them know that it's OK if they grow up to vote differently to you, because we must all vote for who we believe in, regardless of what others do.

Teaching tweens to see bias in the media

The world we live in today gives us instant access to information. Recently, I was speaking to my own teenagers about growing up in an age before the internet, when news and current affairs were restricted to television and newspapers, and how you had to trust the information you were given because there was no other source available to fact check. Life today, and specifically the internet, makes it easier to access impartial and unbiased information, but finding it can sometimes feel like wading through treacle. The tween years are a good time to start a discussion with your child about the validity and reliability of information they access online, hear on the television and read in the printed media. Teaching your tween to approach information with a degree of suspicion is a sad indictment of our times, but an important life skill. The following are good ideas for discussion:

- Ask them if they can see any racist bias in the news. Can they spot headlines that present a racist undercurrent – about refugees, for example?
- As above, see if your tween can spot any homophobic or transphobic articles or news pieces. This could be a commentator on a TV show or stereotyped pictures used to illustrate an article.
- Challenge your tween to search for sexist reporting. You could look at an online newspaper website and ask them to count how many articles include women in bikinis or skimpy clothes, often with criticisms of their appearance, and then compare them to similar articles featuring men.
- Encourage your tween to visit several news sources reporting on the same story. What differences can they

see or hear? Are the viewpoints the same? Have the sources reported the facts and information equally?
- Be careful of the sources you get your own news from as an adult. Try to vary them and point out any problems that you come across to your tween at the time.

Raising your tween to be a media-savvy, objective thinker is a wonderful life skill that is often overlooked. Yet this critical approach can give them a great advantage in their academic studies as they grow, as well as enabling them to develop good analytical skills to help them in almost every aspect of their personal lives.

I'd like to end this chapter with a quote from one of my son's favourite Dr Seuss stories – *The Lorax*:

Unless someone like you cares a whole awful lot, nothing is going to get better. It's not.

The Lorax is a wonderful story about a tween boy who learns the tale of the destruction of nature in a beautiful land, because of corporate greed. The adults, caring only for profit, persist with the destruction until there is nothing of any beauty left. Things change only when the boy, with his passion for nature, learns of the land's plight and saves it, starting with replanting just one tree.

Our tweens are our future. We need them to care about our world and everything in it. The responsibility for that passion, and for raising a generation that cares, lies with us.

Chapter 10

Screen Time and Growing Up Online

'What's society going to be like when the kids today
are phenomenally good at text messaging and spend
a huge amount of on-screen time, but have never
gone bowling together?'

CLIFFORD STOLL, astronomer

The quote above is sobering. Life today for tweens is mark-
edly different from how it was for us. While we spent hours
out on our bikes, calling for friends and playing in fields, woods
or local playgrounds, with perhaps just an hour or two watching
children's television at the end of the day, or playing on slow and
clunky computers and gaming systems, our tweens spend a huge
majority of their free time online. Their leisure world is virtual,
and their friendships and relationships are increasingly formed
through a screen. But does this mean that they are missing out?
Are we looking back at our halcyon days through rose-tinted
spectacles, painting too negative a picture of our tweens online
lives? Or are we right to be worried about the ever-increasing use
of technology by tweens and teens today?

In this chapter, we will take a brief look at some of the current evidence and consider the best way forward for today's tweens. We will also look at the boundaries and rules parents and carers of tweens should consider, to keep them both healthy and safe online.

Is screen time really all bad?

Ironically, the internet is full of articles warning of the dangers of children spending too much time online. Read any item about screen time, particularly in the tween and teen years, and you will come across some scary-sounding statistics. The problem parents and carers have today is trying to make sense of these studies and applying them realistically to their own children.

One ten-year-long study of tweens between the ages of eight and eleven years found that 63 per cent regularly spend at least two hours or more per day using screens recreationally.[1] Add in the time spent on screens at school or doing homework, and it is not unrealistic that this figure would double. From an academic perspective, this usage can be worrying. A review of over 5000 studies, looking at children and adolescents from twenty-three different countries, found that increased time spent watching television, using smartphones, tablets and computers and playing video games, was associated with poorer academic outcomes, particularly in maths and language skills, with the biggest negative effect occurring in the tween years.[2] It isn't just learning that is affected, though. A study of almost 5000 nine- and ten-year-olds found that tweens who had three hours or more screen time per day had a significantly increased risk of obesity and insulin resistance, which, in turn, could increase the risk of the development of type-2 diabetes in later life compared to their peers who had one hour less screen time per day.[3] Screen usage can also have an extremely negative impact on sleep, the blue light emitted inhibiting the secretion of melatonin (the sleep hormone) and the games and activities providing psychological stimulation (making it harder to unwind at night), as well as distorting time (meaning tweens will often stay online for far longer than they had planned). Research has found that 75 per cent of children have screens in their bedrooms and 60 per cent of tweens and teens admit to using these in the hour running up to their regular bedtime.[4] A large review of sixty-seven different studies looking at the screen usage of tweens and teens found that screen time was negatively linked to reduced sleep duration and later bedtimes in 90 per cent of cases.[5]

While screen time can undoubtedly have some negative consequences for our tweens, it isn't all bad. Often, the ill effects can be overstated, particularly when the studies are not looked at with a nuanced view. For instance, a lot of the research around the ill effects of screen usage focuses on television watching but is applied to all screens. Watching television is a naturally passive act that does not require much action or thought from the viewer, whereas playing games or interacting with friends online are vastly different. One study disputing the claim that screen time has dire consequences for tween and teen mental health has shown that screens have little to no effect on their wellbeing.[6]

Screens are, and will continue to be, a vital part of our world and it's important that our tweens grow to be tech savvy, so that they can fully embrace the educational and vocational opportunities available to them. Screen time also carries some benefits for tweens. A recent trial has found that playing a video game is helpful for tweens with ADHD, by improving their attention.[7] Our world has changed and screens now form a major part of socialising; they help tweens to form and maintain relationships, provide inspiration, aid them in their studies and give them a way to relax and switch off from the pressures of the real world for a while. It is naïve to try to avoid screens during the tween years altogether; instead, the best approach is one that is mindful of the pitfalls, while embracing the benefits.

Screen-time rules

The only essential when it comes to screen-time rules for tweens is that you have some. Beyond this, the rules you set need to feel right for you and your child. What is right for one family may not be for another. For rules to be effective they should be reached collaboratively, with your tween's involvement. This provides a sense of ownership and fairness, whereby tweens feel that their voices are valued and heard. You may consider some of the following as a starting point to set your own family rules:

- No screens in the bedroom at night. All devices should be left in a specific place in your main living area instead.
- No screens at the table at mealtimes.
- All homework to be completed before screen usage (unless the screen is needed for the homework).
- No more than one hour at a screen at any one time; regular breaks away from screens to be taken.
- No more than two hours screen time in any one day (excluding usage for schoolwork).
- No screens after 8 p.m. (or one hour before bedtime, if it is earlier or later).
- No purchasing anything online without a discussion with you first. This includes taking out 'free trials' on apps and games, which automatically debit cards if not cancelled by the end of the trial period.
- No downloading apps without a discussion with you first.
- No eating while using screens, to encourage a full focus on eating and a reduction in the likelihood of overeating.

Of course, if you set screen-time rules for your tween, it's only fair that you follow them, too. Remember that you are their role model. There is no point attempting to limit their screen time if you always have your mobile phone in your hand. You need to lead by example, not just with your words. I would also really recommend trying to engage with what your tween does online. For example, you could learn a game that they enjoy and play it with them, challenging them to see who can get the highest score. Or you could film a silly dance together to upload to social media. Enjoying screen time together is a great way to spend one-to-one time with a tween who may need more connection – meeting them in the way they prefer is always more successful.

Screen-time addiction

Many parents worry that their tweens are addicted to screen time. But addiction is a strong word. Ask yourself how your tween is when they are away from screens, say, on a day out or on holiday? Are they agitated, anxious, angry? Does screen time seem to run your family? Does it dictate what you can do at any given time? Does screen-time usage negatively affect your tween's sleep? Their eating? Or does it negatively affect their school performance? If your answers to these are 'no', then it is unlikely that your tween has an addiction to screen time, even though it may feel otherwise at times.

If you are concerned about your tween's screen usage, try to find a calm time to sit and talk to them about its effects – if you notice it makes them angry, for example. You could also talk about the fact that scientists have found that screens impact on sleep and that this can also affect their weight and health in later life. Show them videos about the influence of screens if you can, or memes designed for their age group. It's also a good idea to chat with your tween about their brain (see pages 10–13) and how they are much more likely to find things addictive and have trouble regulating their time on screens compared to adults. Also, that videos games in particular are designed to be addictive and to make them want to spend money with in-app purchases, virtual goody bags, limited-edition skins (character outfits) and the like. Once tweens understand all this they can become more adept at spotting problems and signs they need to take a break. You could also use a parental app to control access to the sites they visit and the time they are allowed online, or use a Wi-Fi timer, so that access is turned off at certain times of the day. Of course, that means it is also off for you, too, which is no bad thing, as most adults could also do with reducing their online time.

Social-media boundaries

Recent surveys have found that social-media usage by tweens and young teens is rising rapidly, with 70 per cent of thirteen-year-olds checking accounts several times every day.[8] The following tips are important for tweens and their parents and carers to consider when using social media:

- Follow the age recommendations for each site; they are there for a reason. For most sites (including Facebook, Instagram, TikTok, Snapchat and WhatsApp) the mini-mum user age is thirteen.
- Keep accounts private. Make sure that your tween's account has the highest security settings and there is no public access to their posts.
- Be careful with usernames and profile photographs. Don't choose a username that includes their real name or a photo that shows their face or any identifiable features.
- Make sure your tween only accepts followers they know in real life.

- Make an agreement that you, as a parent, must be allowed to follow your tween, or be added as a friend.
- Tell your tween that if anybody makes them feel upset or unhappy, they should unfollow or unfriend the person.
- Encourage your tween to speak to you if they ever get a private message or comment that makes them feel uncomfortable, or contact from somebody they don't know.
- Discuss with your tween that even if they delete something, somebody may have already screenshot it. They should never say anything online that they wouldn't want to shout aloud to thousands of people, even if their account or the conversation is private. And remind them that cyberbullying is still bullying (see also page 100).

From a parental perspective, do resist the urge to comment on everything that your tween posts, especially if your words could be embarrassing. As much as you need to trust them, they also need to be able to trust you.

KEEPING SAFE ONLINE

Whatever your tween is doing online, there is a strong chance that they will come across somebody who isn't who they say they are, or who sends them inappropriate photos or comments. Perhaps one of the most important conversations you can have with them about online life is one where you explain that they should never give out any personal information online (which includes, but is not limited to: the name of their school, the town or street they live in, their name or the name of their siblings or parents and their date of birth) and they should never share photos of themselves, or anything that may identify them (for instance, a photograph wearing a school uniform with a logo).

Several charities produce educational videos for parents and carers to use with their tweens, warning of the danger of strangers on the internet. You can find some in the Resources section on page 243. It is also a good idea to keep your tween in the same room as you if they are playing games online where they can speak to people as they play. This way you will be able to listen in for any inappropriate contact. You should also take some time to explain phishing and scams to your tween, making sure they know to never click on a link sent to them via an email, text or private message online. Finally, make sure your tween knows that they can (and should) always come to you if anything they encounter online makes them feel uncomfortable.

Should you share your child's pictures online yourself?

So far, this chapter has focused on what our tweens do and post online, but I think it's important to mention what we post online ourselves, especially if it is concerning our tweens.

We too are living in a new era, where parents share almost every element of their lives online, from pregnancy and birth, to children's birthday parties, sports days, school plays and holidays. I can't help wondering how our tweens will feel when they are older to find their whole childhoods documented online. Will they love that their childhood memories are readily accessible to them, stored for them to view and cherish? Or will they feel embarrassed that their lives are out there, laid bare for all – including classmates, future employers, colleagues and future romantic interests – to see.

There is surely a maze of ethics to navigate here, too. Can our children give truly informed consent for their images to be shared with the world? And should we ask for their go-ahead before we share them? On the latter, I am firmly of the opinion that we should ask our tweens' permission before we post something containing their words or images. And as frustrating as it may be if they refuse, I believe we should honour their wishes. It's an ethical minefield, for sure, and that's without the potential safety issues: how easy would it be to find out where a child lives, based on local landmarks in photographs or identifiable school uniform or bags in pictures that you or relatives share? The thought is too scary to even contemplate.

I'm not suggesting we stop sharing photos of our children, but I do think we need to consider their feelings, both current and future, about how we use them and also the repercussions our sharing may have. I only share photographs showing my children's faces in my personal, private, social-media accounts, where I have a minimal number of 'real-life' friends and family and even then, if they ask me not to share an image, I won't. I'm not suggesting this is the right way for everyone, but I do think we all need to think about it more. After all, if we are asking our tweens to be careful about privacy in their online lives, we must set the bar ourselves.

I am excited for this generation – one that has so many more opportunities than we ever had, with the world literally at their fingertips. I don't believe we should shy away from screens; they are important and will continue to play a significant role in our tweens' futures or even careers. I do believe that usage should be mindful and careful, though. Achieving a good balance is the way forward – something that works for you and your tween and everyone else in your family. Finding your own unique way for you and your family is always the best way.

Chapter 11

School Motivation, Homework and Future Aspirations

'Education is the most powerful weapon which you can use to change the world.'

NELSON MANDELA

The tween years see many changes in education. Gone are the relaxed free movement in classrooms and primary emphasis on learning through play that are so common in the early years. And in their place come more formal teaching, homework and tests. Tweens also need to navigate one of the biggest and, according to research, most stressful life events: the move to secondary school.[1] Once there, their focus needs to shift on to future plans, choosing subjects to study for qualifications that will open up doors to their would-be careers. These changes and challenges can inspire and motivate tweens, making them excited about what the years ahead have in store for them; but they can also bring anxiety, worry and difficult situations, requiring support and skill from parents and carers, as well as the school community.

In this chapter, we will look at the most common school-related issues faced by parents and carers of tweens, from preparing them for the transition to secondary school to coping with homework struggles and empowering tweens to make academic choices for the future.

Preparing for the move to 'big school'

Can you remember how you felt in the months before starting at secondary school? I felt excited, but also worried and scared: fearful of the size of the school in relation to my comparatively tiny primary school, worried about getting lost and anxious that I wouldn't be able to keep up with the work. I was also concerned about making friends and fitting in, frightened I would get the wrong bus home and nervous about navigating lunchtimes in the huge canteen. Of course, my fears were unfounded; within a month, I had formed new friendships, knew my way around easily and was loving the challenge of learning new subjects. The same was true for all my children. But despite knowing that our tweens will be fine, we must not dismiss their fears.

The following are some of the most common anxieties tweens experience before the move to a new school, according to research:[2]

- Making new friends.
- Learning new academic subjects.
- Meeting new teachers.
- Getting used to a new routine.
- The increased size of the new school and the number of children in it.

Whatever worries tweens may have about the transition to a new school, the two most important responses from parents and carers are, firstly, to listen and, secondly, to empower them to cope with their concerns. The following tips can help with the latter:

- Reassure your tween that all new starters will have worries, even those who look cool, calm and collected on the outside. Help them to understand that a degree of apprehension is totally normal with such a big transition ahead of them.
- Give your child a little notebook and suggest that they write down any concerns or questions they have. You can check on their questions every couple of days – or daily, if you think that would be better – and if you don't know the answers immediately, promise you will find out for them as soon as you can.
- Even if the school is running settling-in sessions, ask if you can have a video tour of the building, or at least some photos of your child's new form room and form tutor. Familiarising themselves with these before the beginning of term can help them to feel more comfortable when they start.
- Do let your tween's form tutor and whoever is responsible for student wellbeing know if they are feeling very anxious before starting. Often, schools have special settling-in procedures for tweens who they think will struggle.
- Try to buy any uniform needed several weeks before the start of term, so that your tween can wear it around the house, including new shoes (blisters in the first week aren't fun). If they must wear a tie as part of their new uniform, keep practising at home until they are a pro at tying it.

- See if you can find other new starters and arrange a lunch date with them before term begins. Local social-media groups are good for linking up with other parents.
- Make sure your tween knows where to go and who to ask for help at school if they are lost or feeling out of their depth. Also, check that they know what to do if they feel ill or are in pain (including period pain) while at school. Usually, this will be a visit to the school nurse's office.
- Try to focus on the positives. Ask your tween what they are most looking forward to about starting their new school. Speak about the new opportunities they will have and the activities they love. You could also find out what lunchtime and after-school clubs will be running and share the list with your tween, to build excitement.
- Try to get hold of a map of the school before they start, so they can familiarise themselves with the entrance, their form, the school hall, the canteen and the toilets.
- Do a couple of practice runs of their school journey, especially if your tween will be using public transport or walking.
- Try to get them as organised as possible before starting, checking that they have the right stationery and equipment packed in their bag, so that everything they need will be to hand.
- Give them some coping mechanisms for when things feel a little too much (the tips in Chapter 5 will help – see page 121).

Of course, the above tips have focused solely on helping your tween to cope with the transition to a new school, but it's important not to forget what a big experience it is for you, too. Try to attend any new parents' information evenings and take advantage of offers to chat with form tutors before, or soon after, your tween starts school. Most schools will run a parents' evening towards the end of the first term, which will give you an opportunity to meet your tween's teachers and hear about how they are settling in. I think one of the hardest things about being a parent or carer to a tween at secondary school is having far less involvement with school than you had previously. It feels strange not knowing their teachers well or what room they will be in at any given time. You do get used to the change, but it can often take parents longer than tweens to feel at peace with the transition.

Homework refusal

Secondary school often brings an increase in homework and along with it, more disagreements and stress at home if your tween is reluctant to get it done. I don't think any tweens enjoy all homework and eagerly complete it without any issues – at least not once they're into the second term and beyond. So if you find it hard to get your tween to do their homework, please know that you are not alone.

From a tween's perspective, they've had to cope with a huge upheaval and transition in starting secondary school, the hours can be longer, with a longer commute thrown in and lots more moving around, walking from classroom to classroom. It's understandable, then, that when they come home, the last thing they want to do is more work. Just like you or me after a long day at work, they want to relax (and eat!). For many tweens, relaxing encompasses screen time and, as we know from the previous chapter, this can result in time distortion, meaning they stay online for longer than even they had planned. Then, inevitably, it gets harder to drag them away from the screens to start their homework, the homework builds up until it seems like an insurmountable task and you end up with a very unhappy tween, who will usually tend to do anything to avoid tackling that homework pile. This is all so common, but can be worked around, with the following tips:

- Explain to your tween that you understand they need to relax, but they also need to do their homework. See if you can collaboratively come up with a routine that allows them that important relaxation time and time to do their homework. For instance, you may choose to have a 'homework hour' between 5 and 6 p.m. every day; what they do before and after this time is up to them, but they must do homework between 5 and 6 (unless they don't have any).
- If your tween finds it hard to get off screens once they start, you may consider a boundary that screens only happen after homework is completed.
- Try to set aside some time to sit with them while they work; you could work on your own projects or admin at the same time, setting a good example.
- Make sure they have a drink and a snack before homework time. Most tweens come home from school absolutely famished and find it hard to concentrate before they have eaten.
- Help your tween with their organisational and study skills. Overwhelmed tweens will procrastinate a lot. The key to getting homework done is to avoid overwhelm. Teach them how to prioritise work based on date order (when it is due in) and how to break it down into bite-size individual tasks. Most schools will give out homework diaries, or planners, so you can see the date each piece is due in by. Utilising a simple filing system, with a couple of trays saying, 'Do today' and 'Do tomorrow' can be helpful.
- Check if there are any underlying reasons for their difficulties with the work: do they actually understand what is expected from them? Are they struggling with the

level of work that has been set? In this case, encourage them to contact their teacher and ask for help and a better explanation.

- Don't be afraid to allow them to get into trouble. Most parents and carers are horrified when I say this, but sometimes the absolute best way to get tweens to do something is to allow them to experience the consequences of not doing it. If we always work hard to make sure their homework is completed fully and on time, we help them to avoid the consequences of not doing it. However, those consequences may be the very thing they need to spur them on.

If you do find that your tween is having a hard time with the amount of homework they are set, particularly from one specific teacher, don't be afraid to get in touch with their form tutor or class teacher to discuss your concerns. You shouldn't reach the point where homework is disrupting your home life with any regularity; if it does, you really do need to speak to the school about it.

Coping with tests and exams

While tweens have probably sat for standardised tests at primary school and had in-class spelling and times-table tests and the like, tests and exams at secondary school very much shift things up a gear. This is likely to be the first time that your tween has sat in an exams hall and experienced a glimpse of what the future holds for them. Often, secondary schools will sit pupils for something known as CATs (cognitive ability tests) very soon after starting. These help schools to get a baseline measure of students' cognitive abilities and are often used to sort them into different groups for subjects that may be streamed, like maths.

Not all schools do this, but if your child does need to sit CATs, the best thing you can do is to reassure them that the results don't have a huge impact on their future. Help your tween to see these tests as a way for the school to get to know them a tiny bit, but reassure them that they are not defined by their scores and nor do they tell the school anything about their passions and interests or personality traits. Students will be moved into the classes that best suit them as their schooling continues, so the CATs don't label them for ever more.

When it comes to end-of-year tests, often used to help write reports and set target grades, most tweens will probably benefit from you spending time with them to develop study skills. I remember becoming furious with one of my boys who refused to revise for his school exams, until one day, I had an epiphany. I asked him, 'Do you know how to revise?' He replied, 'No, not really!' We then spent a good couple of hours talking through different ways to revise and how different things work for different people: some prefer to watch revision videos; some like to read books and make notes on small pieces of card; some recite the work aloud, to themselves, or somebody else; some like to make big posters or mind maps of the main facts; some listen to revision notes either they or somebody else has recorded; and some like to use apps and websites, using interactive quizzes and the like. There are so many different revision options open to tweens today that it can seem a little overwhelming – and the result of that overwhelm is no revision! Helping your tween to unravel and reduce their options to the one most appropriate for them is the best way to encourage revision.

On the subject of the best way to revise, I'm regularly asked about my opinion on rewarding exam results. I often hear of parents paying their children a set amount of money for every 'A' grade they receive. I am a huge critic of this approach for the following reasons:

- Rewarding grades encourages a fixed mindset: if tweens don't think they can get the A fairly easily, then they won't try. This then reduces the amount of effort they put in and can mean they get a much lower result than if the reward had never been on offer.
- Rewarding grades focuses on extrinsic (external) motivation. Rather than the child revising hard because they want to achieve a good result for the pride and feeling of accomplishment, they work to get a reward. There are two problems with this: firstly, when the reward is no longer on offer, they stop trying; and secondly, extrinsic motivation actually undermines intrinsic (internal) motivation – that in-built drive to succeed.
- Rewarding based on grades is particularly unfair for children who have a hard time at school and those younger siblings who are not likely to achieve such high grades and will therefore miss out on the rewards given to their more academic older sibling.

But because I don't reward for exam results (or good marks in coursework), it doesn't mean that I ignore the accomplishments of my children. To encourage a growth mindset, I place my praise on their efforts, not their outcomes. I will praise when they are working hard, even if they get a D, rather than focus on an A, which may have come from little effort. To create the best academic outcomes possible for tweens, it's so important to focus on the effort, not the outcome. We also celebrate the end of term and the fact that we have all survived the challenges of school over the previous few months, sometimes with a meal out or an evening at the cinema. So we still celebrate, but we celebrate the accomplishment of getting through a term, rather than fixating on grades and marks or reports.

Picking up on a point mentioned in the homework section previously, my best advice for parents and carers who have a tween who avoids revising for tests and exams, no matter how much you try to help, is to let them fail. Adults often intervene too much with the revision process, helping the tween to scrape through, and while we think we're helping, we're really not. To build that intrinsic motivation to revise, tweens must experience what it feels like to be sitting in a test with that stomach-sinking feeling, thinking, Oh no! I should have revised! They also need to know how it feels to be on the receiving end of test or exam results that are poor when they have not put enough effort in. Of course, when this happens, control your urge to say, 'I told you so' and instead say, 'OK, well, now you know what happens when you don't revise, what can you differently next time?' Allowing your tween to experience failure because of their inaction in the earlier years of secondary school, before the all-important exams later on is crucial, I think, to their future success. Don't fear letting them fail, but instead embrace it mindfully, knowing that any temporary failure will help to build resilience and motivation to succeed more in the future.

Struggles with school discipline

Discipline at secondary school is often a huge change for both tweens and their parents. Gone are golden time, class dojos, traffic-light systems and the like and in their place are detentions (lunchtime and after school), isolation (where children are expected to sit in a room, or booth, away from their peers to complete their work, usually for a half day or full day) and even exclusion, where they are removed from the school either temporarily or permanently. Secondary-school discipline leaves a lot to be desired, being neither mindful of current science nor effective. Sadly, however, a change in school discipline would usually require a huge overhaul of a system that hasn't got the time or the financial capacity for the adjustments needed. This means that parents need to make peace with the school's discipline policy, even if they don't like it.

I would encourage you to meet with your tween's form tutor or head of year to discuss any concerns that you have – but go into the meeting with realistic expectations. The school won't change their whole approach to discipline based on your discussion, but they may agree to look at one small part of it. Here, pick your battles – go for the smallest aspect that bothers you the most, rather than trying to change the world. The most important thing for parents and carers to do in any discussion involving discipline with their school is to be their tween's advocate. Be prepared to stand up for your tween and their rights, even when you feel uncomfortable doing so. Your tween needs you to be their voice and in their corner. See if you can come up with a solution with the school that is as holistic as possible – one that considers the reasons why your child misbehaved, rather than just punishing them for what they did. Often, poor behaviour at school is an indicator that the child needs better learning support. It is not uncommon for tweens to be diagnosed with a special educational need or disability once they start secondary school, the warning signs being their behaviour and problems settling. For this reason, discipline must be relevant to the potential causes of behaviour and involve working as a team – you, your tween and the school – to remove as many obstacles as possible.

If your tween is struggling with their behaviour at school, it's also incredibly important to provide a secure, supportive environment at home. This may mean more difficult behaviour for you, while your tween lets off steam within the safety of home and with those who love and accept them authentically. Indeed, many tweens show behaviour regression at home when they start secondary school but behave like angels at school. I remember several parents' evenings where I didn't recognise the quiet, studious and polite child being described, because their behaviour at home had been so tricky. This restraint collapse (where the tween doesn't feel they need to keep all their big feelings inside) at home is actually a wonderful compliment to your parenting skills. It means your tween feels safe to be who they are, warts and all, around you. This explosion of big feelings at home is often what helps tweens to cope with what's expected of them at school. You have extraordinarily little control over the behaviour policies of your tween's school, but you have total control over how you do things at home.

Undiagnosed SENDs in the tween years

Following on from the previous section, the tween years can often highlight differences between those who are neurotypical and those who are affected by a learning difficulty, more commonly termed SEN (special educational need) or SEND (special educational needs and disabilities). This was the case for one of my children.

I'd had a little inkling he was different to his peers and siblings – he was always getting into more trouble than them at infant and primary school, had some problems with his work and displayed much more erratic and difficult behaviour at home. I mentioned my concerns to his class teacher when he was around six years old and the school decided to call in an educational psychologist to assess him. The conclusion was that he was 'totally normal, but a little immature'. My niggles didn't go away, but the school reassured me there was nothing wrong with him and that he just needed 'stronger discipline' at home and at school – something I heartily disagreed with. Harsh discipline (time out, naughty step, exclusion and the like) and an emphasis on praising and rewarding from the school did nothing to help his behaviour, but did have a hugely negative effect on his self-esteem and confidence. We continued to limp through the school system, and every time I raised concerns I was told, 'the educational psychologist said there is nothing wrong with him'.

When he started secondary school, the gulf between him and his peers widened. Educationally, he was struggling, and emotionally things had reached a critical point. His relationships with his peers were fragile, due to his difficult behaviour, he had no close friends, he was constantly in trouble at school and his grades were slipping. Again, I raised my concerns with the (new) school, and my parenting and so-called 'lack of discipline' were blamed once again. One day, after yet another incident at school (I can't recall exactly what now, there were so many), I remember speaking with my son at home. Something clicked and I asked him, 'Can you behave any better?' and he said, 'No, I can't. I don't know what to do.' It became startlingly apparent to me that he wasn't deliberately 'being naughty' – he was trying his best, but his best was being outwitted by something in his brain that prevented him from behaving as expected.

The next day, we went to our family doctor and I begged for a referral to a paediatric mental-health consultant who specialised in SEND. That consultant turned out to be our saviour. He listened, properly, to my concerns, in a way that nobody had before and, most importantly, he listened to my son, too. After my son, myself and his school were asked many questions, he was finally diagnosed with attention deficit hyperactivity disorder (ADHD) at the age of thirteen. Many discussions later, we all agreed to a trial of medication, which gave his brain better control over his impulses. Within a couple of months, he was like a changed child – calmer, happier, more confident, making new friends – and his grades shot up, too. When I look back now, I am furious at the educational psychologist and the primary school who dismissed my concerns so readily and with his secondary school for continuing to dismiss them for his first two years. I am, however, glad I trusted my instinct and stood my ground, despite effectively being told by apparent expert after expert that I was just a bad parent.

Sadly, our story is all too common. Awareness of SEND is shockingly low, and far too many families struggle through childhood, adolescence and beyond without an appropriate diagnosis, treatment and all-important support. SEND can look different to the stereotypes many teachers, special-educational needs co-ordinators (SENCOs) and even educational psychologists expect. Girls on the autistic spectrum or those with ADHD, for instance, do not tend to present with the typical traits often shown by boys, and many can be misdiagnosed or not diagnosed at all. If you feel instinctively that your tween may be different, listen to that instinct, for it is usually right, and keep pushing for the support that you all deserve. See Resources, page 243, for help.

Future career decisions

It may seem a little pre-emptive to include a section on career decisions in a book about tweens. After all, don't they have at least five years or more before they must start thinking about that sort of thing? Not so. The subjects your child will sit exams in at the age of sixteen usually need to be chosen when they are around twelve or thirteen. The results of these exams will form the basis of the further-education qualifications they can sit for (many have prerequisites) and these, in turn, will dictate the higher-education opportunities available to children (or adults, as they will be by then) at eighteen and beyond. So the subjects your child chooses in their tween years can, and do, impact on their whole future. A scary thought, huh? (I'm still trying to work out what I want to do with my life three decades on, so the thought of a twelve- or thirteen-year-old having to decide what they want to do with the rest of their life seems insane.)

So how can you help your tween? It's never too early to speak about careers that may be of interest to them. They don't need to pin something down exactly, but perhaps they may have an idea of wanting to work with computers, or animals or the arts or building something with their hands ... Even these loose ideas can help to steer their academic options. They should make good use of any careers counselling or experience sessions at school when they are on offer, too, and they should never be afraid of changing their minds; just because they made a decision once, they don't have to stick to it. If your tween has no idea what they want to do (as many don't), then perhaps the best way forward is to keep any course options as broad as possible (including a good mix of subjects from the arts and technology, as well as sciences, languages and humanities), allowing them to go in any direction they choose in the future.

The school years are an integral part of a tween's life. School is often the place where lifelong friendships are made, where future interests are ignited, where hobbies become passions and, hopefully, self-esteem and confidence are built. That said, it's unlikely that your tween will come through these times without the occasional hiccup, or sometimes a mountainous obstacle. As ever, the key to this journey and guiding them on to the next stage of their academic lives is to stand in the wings, offering support, safety and consistency, and to be prepared to stand up and be their advocate when needed. They will make mistakes, and so will you, but you can learn from them together. After all, the best education happens through experience and keeping a growth mindset. That applies to you as a parent, as well as to your tween as a student.

Chapter 12

Raising a Financially Literate Tween

'If I had my choice, every high school would be teaching financial literacy along with math and science.'

GREGORY MEEKS, American politician

Arguably, the way we, as parents and carers, handle our own finances – the example we set to our tweens and what we teach them about money – will be the strongest influence on how they handle their own personal finances as they grow. I've always found it strange, and a little worrying, that this area is omitted from school lessons. After all, it's something we all need to understand as adults and yet our tweens and teens are so ill prepared. I thought I had done a pretty good job when my children were small, until one day, at a festival, my then six- or seven-year-old pointed out a cash machine with a 'Free money withdrawals' sign. He called me over and said, 'Look, Mum – they're giving away free money. Quick, get some out!' I spent the next half-hour explaining bank accounts, credit and debit cards and cash-machine withdrawal fees to him, pointing out that sadly, it wasn't the money that was free, but the withdrawal. Fast-forward a couple of years and I was sitting in the living room watching TV with another of my sons. An advert came on for a home-equity-release company. My son thought it sounded like a great idea and suggested that we should call the company and request they pay us some money. It took several minutes to explain to him that it wasn't quite as simple as calling up and requesting free cash.

The financial pitfalls of the modern-day world are complex and many. From understanding payday loans to interest-free-credit purchases, buy-now-pay-later schemes and companies offering to buy any vehicle (for considerably less than the market value), there is an urgent need for our tweens to understand the financial world they are about to enter into. And yet there is so little formal schooling on these issues. It's vital, then, that parents and carers themselves raise their tweens with a sound financial education.

What does your tween need to know about money?

The best way to discuss money with your tween is to bring it up in discussions that happen organically – say, in response to an advert on TV or a real-life event. If you are mindful of the need to teach your tween about money, you will find plenty of opportunities to naturally talk about it.

Pocket money is an important way for tweens to learn about money experientially, as is giving them the opportunity to earn their own money. We'll look at these ideas a little more later on in this chapter. For now, here's a list of financial topics that I would aim for your tween to understand as they approach their teen years:

- The difference between a credit and a debit card.
- The difference between a credit balance and debt (overdrawn balance).
- The difference between a prearranged and unauthorised overdraft.
- How interest rates work (for purchases and earning interest on savings).
- How to look at how much credit really costs (including payday loans and personal loans).
- The difference between renting a home and buying one (including how mortgages work).
- How to compare the cost of different items and services.
- How discount codes and coupons work and where to find them.
- How to run a monthly budget.
- How to plan savings (especially for an item or activity).
- How taxes work.
- Household bills and a rough idea of their cost.
- How investments work.
- Why gambling is so risky and why they are unlikely to win (including fruit machines, scratch cards and the like).
- How salaries work – how often they are paid and what the average salary is for a full-time worker in the country you live in.
- How sales work in stores and why they often aren't as good as they appear (for instance, how the price of an item might be temporarily raised for a few weeks, so that it can then be cut dramatically for a sale, making the reduction appear more generous than it really is).
- How giving to charity and donations work.

See also Resources, page 243 for more help with financial discussions with your tween.

Pocket money and learning to budget

I believe that giving tweens pocket money is the best way to teach them about the value of money, budgeting, saving and giving. If you don't already give your tween regular pocket money, then I would seriously consider starting as soon as possible. Pocket money also gives tweens the freedom and control to be able to buy what they want, rather than have to ask you for everything, which reduces the 'I-want' requests that parents of tweens are so often plagued with. It also teaches tweens about foreign-currency exchange when they go abroad, and the value of buying good-quality products or saving money by purchasing pre-loved goods.

How much should you give and how often?

The amount of pocket money you give will obviously depend on family finances. There is no set amount that works, but rather what suits your family, depending upon your budget. If budget is less of an issue for you, then look at the sort of things your tween asks to buy and try to align pocket money to this. You want to give enough that they can make small purchases (magazines, trading cards and sweets, for example) easily, but limit the amount so that larger purchases, such as more expensive toys or video games, need to be saved for. Remember that part of the purpose of giving pocket money is that your tween will learn how to budget and save for 'big-ticket' items over several weeks or months.

The timing of giving pocket money will once again be dictated by your family budget. If possible, I'd always suggest giving it monthly. Weekly pocket money is good for younger children who struggle with saving and looking into the future; tweens, however, with their developing hypothetical-thinking skills, are more suited to monthly payments which can teach them to be patient and wait for purchases. The other benefit of giving pocket money monthly is that it mimics what happens in adult life more closely, with monthly pay packets. The sooner your tween learns how to work with a monthly budget, the more easily they will manage their money when they are older and start work.

How should you pay it?

A bank account is a must for tweens, especially if they haven't had one before. I have always transferred pocket money directly to my tweens' bank accounts on the first day of each month, making it easier for them to budget. Many banks provide accounts with linked savings accounts, allowing your tween to transfer money from one to the other. I would also recommend choosing an account that comes with a debit card (usually, they will need to be eleven for this type). Debit cards allow them to pay for items in shops and online, giving them more independence, while also mimicking the financial transactions they will have as an adult. For younger tweens you may consider a pre-paid debit card, which comes with an app (for those who have a phone), very much like an online bank account, or access to yours. These are generally available to children from the age of six, although the downside is that there is usually a small monthly fee attached (compared to a regular child bank account with debit card that is usually free). The benefit here for young children of having a debit card justifies the fee though, in my opinion.

Should pocket money be linked to chores or behaviour?

Pocket money should not be based on your tween's behaviour, as a reward or a treat. It should be unconditional, otherwise it becomes a form of extrinsic motivation, which we know, ultimately, decreases the likelihood of 'good' behaviour in the future. Pocket money should be given to improve a tween's feelings of autonomy and as a way for them to learn about finances before they need to manage them independently in adulthood. The amount of pocket money they get should be the same every month (or week, if you pay it weekly), with no deductions for tricky behaviour and no 'little extras' if they have been particularly 'good'. I'm often asked, 'But adults have to work for their money – isn't that a form of reward?' And the answer is, of course, yes. However, it's not possible for tweens to work in the same way as you; they're not on a level playing field yet. In addition, you don't get rewarded for household chores, so why should your tween? In fact, if you want them to do their chores, we know statistically that they are more likely to do so if they have never been rewarded for them. You want to raise a tween who helps around the house because that's what's expected of them as part of the family, not because they are paid to do so. It's best to see pocket money more as a universal basic income and educational tool than a reward.

What sort of pocket money boundaries should you set?

It's important to set boundaries and rules around pocket money, and to stick to them, so that tweens know exactly what to expect. These boundaries also help to avoid sticky situations and potential arguments. The following are some of those I set with my own tweens, but of course, it's important to set ones that feel right for your own family, so your list may look different:

- Once you have given your tween their pocket money that money is no longer yours. That means you don't get a say in how they spend it. If they want to blow all of it on something you consider a waste of money, or of poor quality, then that is their prerogative. It is important that they learn about value through their own experiences and natural consequences. I think standing back like this and letting them 'waste' their (or what was your) money is the hardest part of giving pocket money. But remember that what you deem a huge waste may be an absolute treasure to your child, so try as hard as you can not to interfere with their choices. Pocket money is all about them having control, so don't undermine them on this.
- Decide exactly what the pocket money is to cover and stick to it. I pay for their clothes, their mobile-phone contracts, any food we eat out when I'm with them, gifts for friends if they are invited to a birthday celebration and all of their after-school clubs and activities and school trips. Pocket money (in my house) is for any items the children want outside of Christmas and birthdays, as well as covering drinks and food if they go into town with a friend (without me) or buying something on the walk home from school. Lastly, it also needs to cover holiday spending money.
- I don't lend money. If my children see something they want that they cannot afford, I don't lend them the money, nor do I make advance payment of pocket money. They have to wait until the next month and save. I know this may sound mean, but otherwise they

wouldn't learn how to budget and save. You don't get advance salary payments as an adult if you see something you'd like seven days before payday, and lending your children money gives them an unrealistic expectation for the future.

- Don't force your tween to donate to charity. This should be something they choose to do of their own accord. Making tweens 'spend, save and give' extrinsically controls their spending. You want them to give to charity because they want to donate, not because you make them. I love shopping in charity shops, visiting them regularly and my children follow suit. The charity shop is always the place they head for first at the start of the month, as a result. If we see a busker in the street and they ask for money, I will ask them if they have any of their own to use, and the same goes for charity collection boxes. They all spontaneously donate to what they deem to be good causes, and these causes are all different, because it's important that they make the choice of where the money goes themselves. If they want to save or spend all their money one month and not give anything, then that's fine with me. There is no pressure to donate.

While our boundaries for pocket money don't change, we do review the amount given if our personal financial circumstances change, and we also increased it a little as the children started secondary school.

Earning extra money

While I think it's essential to give tweens pocket money, I don't believe they should be given so much that they can buy whatever they want, whenever they want. I have always given my children an opportunity to earn extra money, allowing them to build upon their savings or buy something that was otherwise financially out of their reach. They have grown up watching me sell their outgrown clothing and household items in online auctions and via social-media marketplaces and so were eager to follow suit. Every six months or so we all have a sort out of unused and outgrown items, and I will list them for sale on their behalf. Occasionally, we also have a garage – or rather driveway – sale outside our house and sometimes we will pack up everything and set off early on a Sunday morning to take part in a car-boot sale. I keep the money from any of their outgrown clothing (since I buy it in the first place), but anything else of theirs that they sell is money for them to keep.

I will also pay for any odd jobs around the home and garden that are out of the ordinary. These are not the everyday chores that I expect them to do, but jobs such as mowing the lawn or washing the car. We also keep chickens as a family and sell their eggs from a stall on our driveway and sometimes the children collect the eggs, clean them, box them and put them out on the stall. If they do this, then they can keep a proportion of the profits. At thirteen, three of my children also took on a paper round. The pay was diabolical, but they learned the importance of being reliable and working hard to earn extra money each week.

Giving tweens the opportunity to earn a little extra is such an important boost to their self-esteem, as well as providing the obvious material reward.

Raising children to be entrepreneurs

When I look back at my schooling, any talk of careers always assumed that we would work for somebody else. We were trained to be good employees, to gain the grades we needed for future job roles and how to impress those who would employ us at interview. At no point was I taught how to start my own business or work for myself.

My husband and I are both self-employed and our children take pride in our work and know that they too can start up any venture that inspires them. They have also seen the hard work, sweat and tears that go into self-employment, so they have a rounded picture and know that it is a viable and fulfilling option – something I believe more tweens should understand.

Entrepreneurship starts at a young age. Those children who take an extra chocolate bar into school to sell to the highest bidder, or those who take trading-card games to the park with their friend all show the early spark of being future business leaders and owners. Do make sure you nurture these traits in your tween and supplement the conventional careers advice they receive at school. Further and higher education are not the only ways to enjoy a successful financial future.

So many adults today have a poor understanding of personal-finance concepts, and I think this lack of knowledge – among other causes – plays a big part in the levels of personal debt and financial difficulties that many struggle with. We really must not leave our tweens' financial instruction to their formal education because it is severely lacking in schools. I passionately believe that all parents should teach their tweens to be financially literate and allow them to learn to earn, save, spend, donate and budget money in the safety of the family home from a young age. If we don't, we are doing our tweens a huge injustice that may impact them negatively for many years to come.

I hope this chapter has helped you to consider some of the financial information that tweens today so badly need to know, as well as how to start teaching your tween to budget their money, both now and in the future. Now my children are older, they are all masters at saving, budgeting and bargain hunting – skills that are so important for preparing them for adulthood. And this is a good point at which to move on to our final chapter – all about fostering future independence and the art of 'letting go' as children grow.

Chapter 13

Letting Go and Fostering Independence

'We need in love to practise only this: letting each other go. For holding on comes easily – we do not need to learn it.'

RAINER MARIE RILKE,
poet and novelist

When my eldest son was nine, he asked me if he could walk home alone from school. I immediately refused; we lived a mile from school, and I felt that he was just too young. He was understandably unhappy, which made me reflect on my decision. I wondered why I'd automatically said 'No'. Although he was only nine, he was incredibly sensible, we had done the walk hundreds of times together and I knew he was perfectly capable of undertaking the journey by himself. What was I so afraid of? Two fears were at the forefront of my mind. The first was the chance of him being involved in a road-traffic accident when crossing the main road and the second was the fear of him being abducted.

Statistically speaking, children are more at risk of being

involved in a road accident the older they get,[1] eleven- and twelve-year-olds being twice as likely as a ten-year-old to be run over. Why the sudden jump in accidents? Because commonly parents and carers allow their children to walk to and from school unaccompanied for the first time when they start secondary school. Indeed, my own original plan with my son had been just that.

If we don't give a child freedom and trust them from a young age, how can we expect them to suddenly be mature enough to be self-sufficient – with independent school runs, for example – after they have blown out the candles on their eleventh birthday cake? I pondered on this a little and decided that now was the time to give my son more freedom. He walked himself to and from school regularly from that point on, my only proviso being that we spoke again about road safety and that he would never go with anybody who offered him a lift. Speaking of the all-too-common abduction worry, I reflected on my own tween years: at the age of eight, I was allowed out to play all day with my friends: we would roam the streets, parks and local woods unsupervised (and also uncontactable), returning at a specific time for dinner at the end of the day. Speaking to friends with similar-aged children to my son, most agreed that 'the world is a much scarier place now'. We often hear of missing children in the media, and parents and carers are on high alert, scared to let their tweens out of their sight. When you look at the statistics though, you realise our children are not very much more at risk than we were at the same age;[2] we just perceive the world to be more dangerous now and we rein in their freedom as a result.

Psychologist Tanya Byron has spoken widely about the lack of freedom for modern children and her fears for the effect this will have on their lives. She is quoted in an article in the *Guardian*, saying:

We live in an increasingly risk-averse culture, where many children's behaviour is constrained. We raise them and educate them 'in captivity' because of our anxieties. We are continually hypervigilant, as our anxieties are fuelled by stories and images of violent and aggressive crimes. And then we label children as troublemakers or failures because, as a society, we often fail to see their potential.[3]

I believe it is far more dangerous to keep our tweens 'in captivity', never letting them out unsupervised, than it is to allow them to spread their wings, with some mindful guidance from us.

Keeping tweens safe when you're not with them

Fifty-eight per cent of child-abduction attempts are made by those known to the child.[4] Warning tweens about 'stranger danger' is naïve and problematic, as it implies that they can implicitly trust all adults known to them, and sadly, as these figures demonstrate, this isn't the case. Strangers can also play an important part in keeping tweens safe. For instance, if they get lost, or run into trouble when they venture out independently. I prefer to use the term 'tricky people' with tweens, explaining to them that if any adult makes them feel uncomfortable, regardless of whether they are a stranger or not, they should seek help and tell a parent or carer about the interaction as soon as possible.

The following tips can help to keep tweens safe when they are not with you:

- They should always tell you where they are going and where you can find them. If plans change, they should let you know.
- Agree to drop them off at a friend's house to meet up, or

wait with them while they wait for a friend in a public place, rather than them setting off or waiting alone in public for their friend to turn up.

- Consider giving them a mobile phone, so you can contact each other more easily. If they do have a phone, ask them to check in with you when they arrive safely.
- Agree that they must stick to mutually acceptable curfews; if they are going to be late, then they should let you know.
- They should never go anywhere with someone they don't know, regardless of what the person might tell them (for example, if they say, 'Your mum sent me to pick you up').
- Set up a password that only you and your tween know. Agree that you will always give someone the password if you need them to collect your tween in an emergency. If the person in question doesn't know the password, your tween will know that you didn't send them and that they should not go with them, regardless of what they may say.
- If they run into trouble, they should look for a police officer, a store security guard or a mother with young children to ask for help. If they have a phone, make sure they know how to call 999.
- Brush up on their road-safety skills. Don't trust that they still know what to do because they learned them when they were younger.

Mostly importantly though, make sure that your tween knows that they can tell you anything that is worrying them, without fear of repercussions, punishment or ridicule. This is where mindful discipline is so important: if your tween is used to relying on your support when they feel bad – and thus behave poorly – they will hopefully be more likely to confide in you when something potentially risky happens.

What should children be able to do independently by the end of their tween years?

Keeping safe isn't the only thing that tweens need to know about to foster independence. Many tweens (and teens) today miss out on the basic life skills that so many of us took for granted at the same age. We may think we are being kind to our tweens by organising their lives and not burdening them with chores, but we really aren't. If anything, we make their future harder, by not preparing them for the adult world. The following is a list of life skills that I believe most children should have acquired by the end of their tween years:

- Cook a small selection of basic meals.
- Use a washing machine and tumble dryer and know how to hang laundry on a clothes line.
- Use an iron.
- Sew a missing button on to clothing and simple darning of holes.
- Address an envelope and know where to put the postage stamp.
- Pay money into a bank account and withdraw money using a cash machine.
- Make a shopping list, find items in a supermarket and keep to a set budget.
- Catch a bus or train and purchase a ticket.
- Load, turn on and unload a dishwasher.
- Change a light bulb.
- Use a screwdriver and hammer for basic home repairs and flat-pack furniture assembly.
- Write a formal email or letter, including how to start and sign off.

- Call the emergency services.
- Navigate using a map.
- Basic first-aid skills and CPR.
- Tie a tie (especially if required for their school uniform).

These points will look different, depending on the age and abilities of tweens, but I think it's a good list to aim for, if not by the end of the tween years, at least within the early teens.

Coping with emptying nests

The tween years are an odd dichotomy of the intense need your children still have for you as a parent or carer and a pulling away towards independence. Bigger children have bigger problems, and I often felt like the tween years were harder work than toddlerhood. In so many ways, my children still seemed so small and immature, yet I could see how rapidly they were growing, as I marvelled at their skills and increasing abilities and the way their orbit was changing from closely revolving around me to including more and more friends and acquaintances, in ever-increasing circles. This flip-flopping from intense need to seeking independence is hard for parents. You welcome the end of sleepless nights and the diminishing piles of plastic toys, but you mourn their babyhood and pride gives way to small stabbing feelings of loss.

Looking back, I realise there were many occasions when I had convinced myself that my tweens needed me more than they did really, but they thrived without me more and more. I expected there to be a finite sign that it was time to let go, but there wasn't one. Instead, we need to learn to trust our tweens, as well as our instincts – because sometimes our instincts are confused by the fear of letting go. After all, authoritative parenting is as much about independence as it is dependence, but my word, is it hard!

Just as we begin to find our place in life, so it changes again. It's so much easier to grow roots than to give wings.

How do we learn to let go and trust? Ultimately, we come full circle. We started this book with talking about your own thoughts, feelings and behaviour and how it affects your tween, and we end it with you, too. Nurturing the growth of wings involves being mindful that our fears and worries aren't holding our tweens back and trusting them and everything we have taught them. Try to see your new-found freedom as something to embrace. The tween years are a great time for you to take up a new hobby. Or do as we did (as did many of our friends with children of similar ages): get a dog. The dog soon became the new baby of the family, a focus for my excess nurturing skills and company when my tweens' social lives rapidly outgrew mine. Try to see this time as a job well done. Don't mourn the past; congratulate yourself for the present and look forward to the future with enthusiasm – because your tween's journey has just begun, with so many exciting possibilities ahead of them, thanks to you.

A Closing Note

I hope that this book has provided you with an insight into the years to come and a greater understanding of the issues you may already be facing. The tween years can seem confusing, for parents and carers and tweens alike, but if ever you are unsure about the correct response or way to handle a situation, remember, you were a tween once, and it's likely you already know the answer deep down. Just ask yourself, 'What would I have liked to have happened in a similar situation at that age?' If you're still feeling stumped, remember the TWEEN acronym in Chapter 2:

- Tolerant
- Warm
- Empathetic
- Empowering
- Nurturing

Tweens need us to be tolerant of them, to understand that their brains aren't like ours and still have many years of maturing ahead. They need warmth and unconditional love, especially when they're behaving in unlovable ways, or feeling as if the world is against them. They need us to empathise with them: to put ourselves into their shoes and consider their feelings, even (and especially) when they don't seem to be considering ours. They need us to empower them, to encourage independence and to be their advocates. And finally, they need us to nurture them – perhaps not in the same way we did when they were younger, but they need us just as much now, perhaps even more.

Of course, nobody is perfect. There will be days when you struggle, days when you lose your temper and days when, frankly, you don't want to be around your tween. And that's OK. Take the time to meet your own needs and make space, so that you have space for your tween's needs, too (remember my cornflake analogy – see page 50). Be mindful of your own behaviour – because who you are is likely who your tween will become – but don't be afraid to make mistakes, so long as you learn from them. If you've read this book, I'm quite sure you're already a wonderful parent and your tween is lucky to have you! Be confident in your abilities, as well as those of your tween.

I'd like to close with a quote from the Dalai Lama that I think sums up the goal of parents during the tween years:

Give the ones you love wings to fly, roots to come back and reasons to stay.

I hope this book has helped you to do just that.
Good luck!

Sarah

References

Introduction

1   Protzko, J. and Schooler, J., 'Kids these days: Why the youth of today seem lacking', *Science Advances* (2019), 5(10).
2   National Statistics, 'Smoking, Drinking and Drug Use Among Young People in England', NHS Digital (2019).
3   https://www.childtrends.org/indicators/teen-pregnancy. Accessed online 26 June 2020.

Chapter 1

1   Giedd, J. N., Blumenthal, J., Jeffries, N., et al., 'Brain development during childhood and adolescence: a longitudinal MRI study', *Nature Neuroscience* (1990), 2(10), pp. 861–3.
2   Lu, L. and Sowell, E., 'Morphological development of the brain: what has imaging told us?' In: Rumsey, J. M. and Ernst, M. (eds), *Neuroimaging in Developmental Clinical Neuroscience*, Cambridge University Press, Cambridge (2009).
3   Wahlstrom, D., Collins, P., White, T. and Luciana, M., 'Developmental changes in dopamine neurotransmission in adolescence: Behavioral implications and issues in assessment', *Brain Cognition* (Feb. 2010), 72(1), p.146.
4   Brumellte, S., McGlanaghy, E., Bonnin, A. and Oberlander T., 'Developmental changes in serotonin signaling: Implications for early brain function, behavior and adaption', *Neuroscience* (Feb. 2017), 342, pp. 212–31.
5   Crowley, S., Acebo, C. and Carskadon, M., 'Human puberty: Salivary melatonin profiles in constant conditions', *Developmental Psychobiology* (May 2012), 54(4), pp. 468–73.

6 MacLean, P., 'The triune brain, emotion, and scientific bias. In the Neurosciences Second Study Program', Rockefeller University Press, New York (1970).

7 Sowell, E., Thompson, P., Holmes, C., et al., 'In vivo evidence for post-adolescent brain maturation in frontal and striatal regions', *Nature Neuroscience* (1999), 2, pp. 859–61.

8 Carskadon, M., 'Maturation of processes regulating sleep in adolescents'. In: Marcus, C. L., Carroll, J. L., Donnelly, D. F. and Loughlin, G.M. (eds), *Sleep in Children: Developmental Changes in Sleep Patterns*, (2nd edition), Informa Healthcare (2008), pp. 95–109.

9 Roenneberg, T., Kuehnle, T., Pramstaller P., et al., 'A marker for the end of adolescence', *Current Biology* (2004), 14, pp. 1038–9.

10 Thacher, P. and Onyper, S., 'Longitudinal outcomes of start time delay on sleep, behavior, and achievement in high school', *Sleep* (2016), 39(2), pp. 271–81.

11 Morganthaler, T., Hashmi, S., Corft, J., et al., 'High school start times and the impact on high school students: What we know, and what we hope to learn', *Journal of Clinical Sleep Medicine* (2016), 12(12), pp. 1681–9.

12 Swerdloff, R. and Sinha Hikim, A., in *Hormones, Brain and Behavior* (2nd edition) (2009), Elsevier.

13 Paul, M., Probst, C., Brown, L., et al., 'Dissociation of puberty and adolescent social development in a seasonally breeding species', *Current Biology* (2018), 2;28(7), pp. 1116–23.

14 Vermeersch, H., T'Sjoen, G., Kaufman, J., et al., 'The role of testosterone in aggressive and non-aggressive risk-taking in adolescent boys', *Hormones and Behaviour* (2008), 53(3), pp. 463–71.

15 Marshall W. A and Tanner J. M., 'Variations in pattern of pubertal changes in girls', *Archives of Disease in Childhood* (1969), 44(235): pp. 291–303; Marshall W. A. and Tanner J. M., 'Variations in the pattern of pubertal changes in boys', *Archives of Disease in Childhood* (1970), 45(239), pp. 13–23.

16 Richards, Julia E. and Scott Hawley, R., in *The Human Genome* (3rd edition) (2011).

17 Brix, N., Ernst, A., Lauridsen, L., et al., 'Timing of puberty in boys and girls: A population-based study', *Pediatric and Perinatal Epidemiology* (2019), 33(1), pp. 70–78.

18 The American College of Obstetricians and Gynecologists, 'Menstruation in girls and adolescents: Using the menstrual cycle as a vital sign', Committee Opinion no. 651 (2017).

19 Brix. N., Ernst, A., Lauridsen, L., et al., op. cit.
20 Leonardi, A., Cofini, M., Rigante, D., et al., 'The effect of bisphenol A on puberty: A critical review of the medical literature', *International Journal of Environmental Research and Public Health* (2017), 14(9), p. 1044.
21 Jung, M., Choi, H., Junghwan, S., et al., 'The analysis of endocrine disruptors in patients with central precocious puberty', *BMC Pediatrics* (2019), 19, p. 323; Partsch, C. and Sippell, W., 'Pathogenesis and epidemiology of precocious puberty: Effects of exogenous oestrogens', *Human Reproduction Update* (2001), 7(3), pp. 292–302.
22 Kim, E., 'Long-term effects of gonadotropin-releasing hormone analogs in girls with central precocious puberty', *Korean Journal of Pediatrics* (Jan. 2015), 58(1), pp. 1–7.

Chapter 2

1 Baumrind, D., 'Current patterns of parenting authority', *Developmental Psychology* (1971), 4(1, pt 2), pp. 1–103.
2 Maslow, A. H., 'A theory of human motivation', *Psychological Review* (1943), 50(4) , pp. 370–96.
3 Bion, W., *Attention and Interpretation*, Tavistock Publications (1970).

Chapter 4

1 Graber, R., Turner, R. and Madill, A., 'Best friends and better coping: Facilitating psychological resilience through boys' and girls' closest friendships', *British Journal of Psychology* (2015), 107(2), pp. 338–58.
2 The Children's Society, 'The Good Childhood Report' (2019).
3 George, R. and Brown, N., 'Are you in or are you out? An exploration of girl friendship groups in the primary phase of schooling', *International Journal of Inclusive Education* (2010), 4(4), pp. 289–300.
4 Ng-Knight, T., Shelton, K., Riglin, L., et al., 'Best friends forever? Friendship stability across school transition and associations with mental health and educational attainment', *British Journal of Educational Psychology* (2019), vol. 89(4), pp. 585–99.
5 Simpson, L., Douglas, S. and Schimmel, J., 'Tween consumers: catalog clothing purchase behavior', *Adolescence* (1998), 33, p. 637.

6 Ditch the Label, The Annual Bullying Survey, 2019.

7 Juvonen, J. et al., 'Extending the school grounds? Bullying experiences in cyberspace', *Journal of School Health* (2008), 78(9), p. 496.

Chapter 5

1 The World Health Organization, 'Caring for children and adolescents with mental disorders: Setting WHO directions', Geneva: World Health Organization (2003); Kessler, R., Berglund, P., Demler, O., et al., 'Lifetime prevalence and age-of-onset distributions of DSM-IV disorders in the National Comorbidity Survey Replication', *Archives of General Psychiatry* (2005), 62(6), pp. 593–602.

2 Quidbach, J., Gruber, J., et al., 'Emodiversity and the emotional ecosystem', *Journal of Experimental Psychology: General* (2014), 143(6), pp. 2057–66.

3 Ong, A., Benson, L., et al., 'Emodiversity and Biomarkers of Inflammation', *Emotion* (2018), 18(1), pp. 3–14.

4 Office for National Statistics, 'Suicides in the UK: 2018 registrations' (2019).

5 Chaplin, T., 'Gender and emotion expression: A developmental contextual perspective', *Emotion Review* (2015), 7(1), pp. 14–21.

6 O'Neal, E., Plumert, J. and Peterson, C., 'Parent–child injury prevention conversations following a trip to the emergency department', *Journal of Pediatric Psychology* (2016), 41(2), pp. 256–64.

7 Dweck, Carol S., *Mindset: How You Can Fulfil Your Potential* (2012), London: Robinson.

8 BBC *Newsround* Climate Change Anxiety Survey, https://www.bbc.co.uk/newsround/51451737. Accessed online 3 August 2020

9 https://www.huffingtonpost.co.uk/entry/kate-middleton-childrens-_n_6699266

Chapter 7

1 Lowes, J. and Tiggemann, M., 'Body dissatisfaction, dieting awareness and the impact of parental influence in young children', *British Journal of Health Psychology* (2003), 8(2), pp. 135–47.

2 Ackard, D. and Peterson, C., 'Association between puberty and disordered eating, body image, and other psychological

variables', *International Journal of Eating Disorders* (2001), 29(2), pp. 187–94.

3 Garbett, K. and Diedrichs, P., 'Improving uptake and engagement with child body image interventions delivered to mothers: Understanding mother and daughter preferences for intervention content', *Body Image* (2016), 19, pp. 24–7.

4 Birch, L. and Davison, K., 'Family environmental factors influencing the developing behavioral controls of food intake and childhood overweight', *Pediatric Clinics of North America* (2001), 48(4), pp. 893–907.

5 Carper, J., Orlet Fisher, J. and Birch, L., 'Young girls' emerging dietary restraint and disinhibition are related to parental control in child feeding', *Appetite* (2000), 35(2) , pp. 121–9.

6 Jansen, E., Mulkens, S. and Jansen, S., 'Do not eat the red food!: Prohibition of snacks leads to their relatively higher consumption in children', *Appetite* (2007), 49(3) , pp. 572–7.

7 Newens, K. and Walton, J., 'A review of sugar consumption from nationally representative dietary surveys across the world', *Journal of Human Nutrition and Dietetics* (2016), 29(2), pp. 225–40.

8 Duyff, R., Birch, L., et al., 'Candy consumption patterns, effects on health, and behavioral strategies to promote moderation: Summary report of a roundtable discussion', *Advances in Nutrition* (2015), 6(1), pp. 139S–46S.

9 Joseph, N., Nellivanil, M., Rai, S., Kotian, S., Ghosh, T. and Singh, M., 'Fast food consumption pattern and its association with overweight among high school boys in Mangalore City of southern India', *Journal of Clinical and Diagnostic Research* (2015), 9(5) , pp.13–17.

10 Sadler, R., Clark, A., Wilk, P., O'Connor, C. and Gilliland, J., 'Using GPS and activity tracking to reveal the influence of adolescents' food environment exposure on junk food purchasing', *Canadian Journal of Public Health* (2016), 107 (suppl. 1), p. 5346.

11 Uribe, R. and Fuentes-Garcia, A., 'The effects of TV unhealthy food brand placement on children. Its separate and joint effect with advertising', *Appetite* (2015), 91, pp. 165–72.

12 Freeman, B., Kelly, B., Baur, L., Chapman, K., Chapman, S., Gill, T. and King, L., 'Digital junk: food and beverage marketing on Facebook', *American Journal of Public Health* (2014), 104(12), pp. 56–64.

13 Isasi, C., Ostrovsky, N. and Wills, T., 'The association of

emotion regulation with lifestyle behaviors in inner-city adolescents', *Eating Behaviour* (2013), 14(4), p. 518.

14 Slater, A. and Tiggemann, M., 'Little girls in a grown-up world: Exposure to sexualized media, internalization of sexualization messages, and body image in 6-9-year-old girls', *Body Image* (2016), 18, pp. 19–22.

15 Turner, P. and Lefevre, C., 'Instagram use is linked to increased symptoms of orthorexia nervosa', *Eating and Weight Disorders* (2017), 22(2), pp. 277–84.

Chapter 9

1 Thunberg, G., *No One Is Too Small to Make a Difference* (2019), Penguin.

Chapter 10

1 Walsh, J., Barnes, J., Jameason, C., et al., 'Associations between 24-hour movement behaviours and global cognition in US children: a cross-sectional observational study, *Lancet* (2018), 2(1), pp. 783–91.

2 Adelantado-Renau, M., and Cavero-Redondo, I., 'Association between screen media use and academic performance among children and adolescents: A systematic review and meta-analysis', *Journal of the American Medical Association: Pediatrics* (2019), 173(11), pp. 1058–67.

3 Nightingale, C., Rudnicka, A., Donin, A., et al., 'Screen time is associated with adiposity and insulin resistance in children', *BMJ: Archives of Diseases in Childhood* (2016), 102(7).

4 Buxton, O., Chang, A., Spilsbury, J., et al., 'Sleep in the modern family: Protective family routines for child and adolescent sleep', *Sleep Health* (2015), 1(1), pp. 15–27; Hysing, M., Pallesen, S., Stormark, K., et al., 'Sleep and use of electronic devices in adolescence: results from a large population-based study', *BMJ Open* (2015), 5(1).

5 Hale, L. and Guan, S., 'Screen time and sleep among school-aged children and adolescents: a systematic literature review', *Sleep Medicine Review* (2015), 21, pp. 50–58.

6 Orben, A. and Przybylski, A., 'Screens, teens, and psychological well-being: Evidence from three time-use-diary studies', *Psychological Science* (2019), 30(5).

7 Kollins, S., DeLoss, D., Cañadas, E., et al., 'A novel digital intervention for actively reducing severity of paediatric ADHD

(STARS-ADHD): a randomised controlled trial', *Lancet* (2020), 2(4), pp. 168–78.

8 Common Sense Media, 'Social media, social life: Teens reveal their experiences' (2018), https://www.commonsensemedia.org/research/social-media-social-life-2018.

Chapter 11

1 Coelho, A. and Romão, M., 'Stress in Portuguese middle school transition: a multilevel analysis', *Spanish Journal of Psychology* (2016), 19 (61).
2 Zeedyk, S., Gallacher, J., Henderson, M., et al., 'Negotiating the transition from primary to secondary school: Perceptions of pupils, parents, and teachers', *School Psychology International* (2003), 24, pp. 67–79.

Chapter 13

1 The AA Motoring Trust, 'The facts about road accidents and children', www.theaa.com/staticdocs/pdf/aboutaa/child_safety.pdf.
2 Newiss, G. and Traynor, M-A., 'Taken: A study of child abduction in the UK', Parents and Abducted Children Together (PACT) and the Child Exploitation and Online Protection Centre (CEOP) (2013).
3 Byron, T., 'We see children as pestilent', *Guardian*, 17 March 2009.
4 Newiss, G. and Traynor, M-A., op. cit.

—

Resources

Sarah Ockwell-Smith's website and blog: www.
sarahockwell-smith.com
Sarah Ockwell-Smith on Facebook: www.facebook.com/
sarahockwellsmithauthor
Sarah Ockwell-Smith on Twitter: www.twitter.com/
thebabyexpert
Sarah Ockwell-Smith on Instagram: www.instagram.com/
sarahockwellsmith

Puberty and development

- DSD Families (support for children, young people and families affected by differences of sex development): www. dsdfamilies.org

Recovering from narcissistic parenting

- The Echo Society (support services to those impacted by narcissistic abuse): www.theechosociety.org.uk
- My Horrid Parent (support to navigate the often isolating relationship with a difficult parent): www. myhorridparent.com

Mindfulness for tweens

- Relax Kids (mindful and relaxation techniques alongside positive psychology): www.relaxkids.com
- Youth Mindfulness (charity devoted to developing and delivering mindfulness programmes for children, adolescents and young adults): www.youthmindfulness.org

Bullying help

- Bullying UK (advice and support for dealing with bullying – includes a template letter you can send to your child's school about bullying): www.bullying.co.uk
- RespectMe (Scotland's anti-bullying service): www.respectme.org.uk

Mental health for tweens organisations

- Action for Children (supporting young people experiencing mental-health and emotional wellbeing problems): www.actionforchildren.org.uk
- Anxiety UK (support for children and young people experiencing anxiety): www.anxietyuk.org.uk
- Beat (the UK's eating disorder charity): www.beateatingdisorders.org.uk
- LifeSigns (self-injury advice and support network): www.lifesigns.org.uk
- Mind (support for anyone experiencing a mental-health problem): www.mind.org.uk
- National Centre for Eating Disorders (help and treatment for sufferers of eating disorders): www.eating-disorders.org.uk
- No Panic (helpline for young people who suffer panic attacks and other anxiety-related disorders): www.nopanic.org.uk

- Papyrus (prevention of young suicide): www.papyrus-uk.org
- Place2Be (improving children's mental health; counselling, support and information): www.place2be.org.uk
- Samaritans (providing emotional support to anyone in emotional distress, struggling to cope or at risk of suicide): www.samaritans.org
- Selfharm UK (information for parents on self-harming behaviour): www.selfharm.co.uk
- Young Minds (advice to anyone worried about a child's or young person's behaviour, emotional wellbeing or mental-health condition, up to the age of twenty-five): www.youngminds.org.uk

LGBTQ+

- Gendered Intelligence (trans-led charity working across the UK, aiming to increase understandings of gender diversity): www.genderedintelligence.co.uk/
- NHS Gender Identity Development Service: www.gids.nhs.uk
- Stonewall (organisation campaigning for the equality of lesbian, gay, bi and trans people across Britain): www.stonewall.org.uk

Body autonomy

- NSPCC (how to teach children the PANTS rule): https://www.nspcc.org.uk/keeping-children-safe/support-for-parents/pants-underwear-rule/

Talking to tweens about race (and resources for examining your own attitudes)

- Embrace Race (anti-racism information for parents): www.embracerace.org

- Guide to Allyship (an open-source starter guide): www. guidetoallyship.com/
- Eddo-Lodge, R., *Why I'm No Long Talking to White People About Race* (2017), Penguin
- Kendi, I. X., *How to Be an Antiracist* (2019), Bodley Head

Talking to tweens about homophobia and transphobia

- Families and Friends of Lesbians and Gays: https://www.fflag.org.uk/

Raising a feminist tween

- Chimamanda Ngozi Adichie, *Dear Ijeawele: a Feminist Manifesto in Fifteen Suggestions* (2018), Fourth Estate
- Elena Favilli and Francesca Cavallo, *Good Night Stories for Rebel Girls* (2017), Particular Books

Screen time help for parents

- Internet Matters (not-for-profit organisation empowering parents and carers to keep children safe in the digital world): www.internetmatters.org/
- NetAware (keeping children safe online): www.net-aware.org.uk/
- NSPCC Online Safety Guide: www.nspcc.org.uk/ keeping-children-safe/online-safety/

SEND resources

- Autism UK: www.autism.org.uk
- The UK ADHD Partnership: www.ukadhd.com
- Ipsea (Independent Provider of Specialist Education Advice): www.ipsea.org.uk

- The Dyslexia Association: www.dyslexia.uk.net

Financial education resources

- Money Advice Service (free, impartial money advice and guidance on helping your kids): www.moneyadviceservice.org.uk/en/corporate/you-your-kids-and-money

Index

Note: page numbers in **bold** refer to diagrams.

PINK 12-05-21

PILLGWENLLY